Distributed in the United States by

GlaxoSmithKline

One Franklin Plaza, Philadelphia, Pennsylvania 19101

ISBN Number: 0-9779604-0-4

Printed in the United States of America

Publisher: GlaxoSmithKline

A few years ago, one of the most prestigious management consulting firms showed up at our doorstep. They had been engaged by management to guide Pitney Bowes in restructuring the corporate entity. The consultant proposed that we cut the budget of our benefit function by $4 million. They recommended paring down to a bare-bones staff of low-level benefit managers, explaining that it was the standard matrix—what many other companies were doing. In a quick conversation, I replied that in any given year our health benefit planning function saves Pitney Bowes in excess of $20 million, and even though we're spending multiple millions of dollars, our return on investment is approximately 5:1.

I have a different perspective than many other CEOs regarding health benefits. In any given year, our company is spending $150 million toward the health care of employees and dependents, and naturally we want to manage these costs. But at the same time we aim to achieve value from our health benefits by providing value to employees, customers, and shareholders.

Achieving top value means more than administering claims to the satisfaction of employees; and, it means going beyond the standard paradigm of controlling direct medical care costs. Rather, obtaining value requires an unwavering focus on health as an outcome, and on high-quality, affordable care as the means. Better health, we have learned, is actually better for the bottom line.

My own, initial investigation into value-based benefits design was strongly influenced by an audiotape I heard some years ago, in which Dartmouth professor John E. Wennberg, M.D., discussed outcomes-based health care. Medicine doesn't follow the laws of economics, Wennberg explained. Normally, when supply exceeds demand prices go down; but in medicine when the supply of a particular medical specialty grows in a given community, demand grows with it and prices increase as well. At the same time, health outcomes don't necessarily improve. Medical practice trends are generally localized, he explained, and they tend to adhere to the philosophies of influential providers such as local teaching hospitals and leading physicians.

Listening to that audiotape, it struck me that there's no clear cause-and-effect relationship between money and health. There are many things that improve health that don't cost money, and there are many high-cost health interventions that don't improve health. Therefore, some other factors must be in play. I decided it was in Pitney Bowes' interest to stop focusing exclusively on cost and start uncovering and addressing those factors.

As senior vice president and chief human resources officer Johnna Torsone said recently, "I have not looked for an administrator of health care benefits. I'm looking for a strategist." Under Johnna's aegis, authors Jack Mahoney and David Hom have gained national distinction for their groundbreaking benefits designs. They took an educated gamble in making certain high-value prescription medications more accessible to chronically ill employees, and the gamble paid off not only in better health, but also in a net reduction in pharmaceutical and other health care and disability costs. The thinking behind this strategy is presented in detail in Rule 5.

Jack and David's book goes much farther from the start, however, in laying out a credible, rules-based guide to a sea change in our country's approach to employee health and health benefits. It is my hope that this book will end up on the desks of every CEO, CFO, HR manager, benefit manager, and benefit plan administrator in the United States, both in government and private industry. Unfortunately, it is beyond the scope of this book to address the urgent need of some 45 million uninsured Americans for access to affordable, quality health care.[1] Yet, if more employers and health care plans placed value on health as Pitney Bowes does—and the seven rules presented here are very doable—I believe we could begin to reverse the current trends of health care inflation and strengthen our country's position in the global economy.

U.S. employers have to face the fact that we have a very different and more intractable kind of medical cost crisis than we did 30 years ago. In some respects, we're better off, and in others we're worse off. For example, many diseases that once spelled a death sentence are now increasingly viewed as chronic illnesses, and the costs of treating them, in some cases, actually have decreased. Centers for excellence in cancer care are achieving better outcomes than ever. On the negative side, we have an epidemic of problems related to chronic diseases such as diabetes, heart disease, and asthma. About 78 percent of our health care costs are related to chronic illness, and that number will continue to rise.[2] Obesity and diabetes are increasing significantly in young people, meaning our workforce of the future is going to be beset with multiple chronic conditions. Within the next 10 to 15 years, this could become a crisis the likes of which our country has never seen.

As chronic illness becomes more prevalent, the solutions become much more difficult, because they depend more on encouraging individuals to take care of their own health in partnership with nurses, technicians, and other nonphysician providers. For example, having an MRI test will not help an employee deal with Type 2 diabetes. Nor will injecting more money into the health care system for additional physicians or hospital beds. Managing diabetes requires the person to self-administer insulin shots or other medications, adopt a healthier diet, and engage in regular exercise. Self-management is a challenge for anyone, and the majority of people facing it tend to have lower income and educational levels, and live in communities with limited support systems.

It's a sad reality that our health care system disproportionately allocates resources to treating disease while ignoring the power and effectiveness of primary prevention, health-risk management, and self-management in avoiding and managing chronic health conditions. Decision-makers in many ways are blind to the considerable human and financial benefits of investing in future health.

At the same time, health signifies far more than lower costs for doctors' visits and hospital stays. It's a key ingredient in driving organizational growth and success. People who don't feel well simply don't perform as well. Healthy people have higher productivity and are happier on the job, and this shines through to the way they deal with customers and fellow employees. I've observed this rule in action through my entire business career.

For all these reasons, it becomes the employer's mandate to change how health care is positioned by health plans and how it is perceived by employees, and this means viewing it ourselves from a smarter, more innovative perspective.

I like to say that no one knows how to push the envelope better than Pitney Bowes does, and that's as true in benefit management as it is in any other area of the company. With annual revenues of $5.5 billion, Pitney Bowes is the world's leading provider of mailstream hardware, software, systems and services. The company is as great today as it has been at anytime in its 86-year history, which is something not many employers can say. I believe we're a great company because we use our resources a lot more intelligently than many other organizations do. Specifically in the health area, we are not reducing benefits or shifting costs to employees out of hand, nor are we throwing a lot of money at doctors and hospitals for the sake of increasing their income; rather, we are focused on injecting money into the system in a way that maximizes health. We look at every decision in health care benefits design as a long-term investment in higher productivity and improved cost-efficiency.

The term total value almost could be considered a carryover from what Pitney Bowes has been offering for many long years. It's the notion that we're not always going to be the lowest-cost option in products and services, but over the life of the relationship we will provide greater value to our customers. When it comes to our employees, if we are providing them with a higher level of health, which may cost a bit more up front, the net value to each of us is higher than if we restricted access to appropriate, high-quality health care.

Through new benefits designs and pricing strategies, we are finding that we actually can influence people's health in a positive way. We can help ensure they obtain the most appropriate, evidence-based treatment for their acute and chronic conditions. Using sophisticated data-driven decision making, we can assess the consequences of benefits design in driving people's behaviors, predict our future high-cost areas, and then adjust accordingly. We tend to take a longer time horizon in benefits design—and in assessing behavioral impact—than other companies do. And when targeting our interventions, we take into account not only direct medical costs, but also the impact of poor health on the costs of absenteeism and short-term disability.

A few other employers are doing even more than we are in some areas, and we learn from them. With a widely dispersed work force, we need to develop better methods to link these employees to the health programs that we know are effective. And we need to work even harder to encourage our part-time employees to embrace the lifestyle changes that will enhance their health today and into the future.

What is clear is that there is starting to be a significant change in focus toward the value of health. The following seven rules promise to help sharpen that focus considerably.

Michael J. Critelli
Chairman and CEO
Pitney Bowes

Table of Contents

Acknowledgments

How do you say thanks to so many people who have created the inspiration to write a book on health care for employers? Over the past decade, we have talked to a cadre of key stakeholders representing the health care industry, the employer community, and our own employees. Lessons learned from these interactions have helped us develop an evolving model of value-based employee health benefits. This book is our attempt to articulate these ideas while encouraging other organizations to follow.

The support received from senior Pitney Bowes management in developing and implementing the concepts in this book was incalculable. We would like to give special recognition to our Chairman and CEO, Mike Critelli, and the Senior VP of H.R., Johnna Torsone for their ongoing encouragement and willingness to listen to our "out of the box" ideas.

Next, we would like to thank GlaxoSmithKline for leading the way to understanding the important role employers play in managing today's health care crisis. We are grateful to the team of Fran Molettieri, Kim Gaskin, Nancy Kuhn, Scott Smith, Dana Lawlor, and especially Iris Hill for championing this program.

We also thank George Pfeiffer and Polly Turner of The WorkCare Group, Inc., who provided conceptual guidance and editorial support.

Finally, our special personal thanks:

Jack Mahoney: I would like to recognize Christine Berman, Mary Bradley, Jan Murnane, Celeste Perilli, and Brent Pawlecki, M.D. for their creativity, willingness to challenge ideas, and incredibly dedicated work translating these ideas into concrete and meaningful programs and services for our employees. Also, I'd like to recognize my assistant, Cathy Brukhardt, for her incredible patience and willingness to make "just one more change" to the material. Finally, add to this the mental stimulation and support of David Hom and the working environment is complete.

David Hom: I do not know how I could have done this without the support of my wife, Judy, and our children, Marisa and Mitchell. Also, to my sister Judy-and her legacies Darci and Danny, and husband Tom Tormey-whose beautiful life and fight with cancer inspired me to address the issues presented herein.

Total Value/Total Return
Seven Rules for Optimizing Employee Health Benefits for a Healthier and More Productive Workforce

THE POINT OF RED LIGHT *darted across the screen and landed on the words "three-tiered drug plans."*

George's eyes darted to the clock on the wall, but the minute hand had hardly moved. His thumbs fiddled at his personal digital assistant. If George could catch the earlier flight out, he would miss the glut of traffic and be home in time to kiss his son goodnight. Tomorrow there were more fires to put out at the office. Maybe he'd set fires instead—to all the paperwork on his desk. All the forms. Urgent phone and email messages. Unresolved health care issues. The thought of it all was making his eyelids so heavy.

"… and the cost-saving advantages of instituting tighter formularies," the speaker droned on, aiming his laser pointer at the next PowerPoint® chart.

George had been the benefits director for Nuts & Bolts Manufacturing for a dozen years, and in that time he'd attended a dozen benefits conferences. He wanted to be here. He had to be here—the company's survival depended on it. This year, Nuts & Bolts was facing an unprecedented 15 percent increase in employee health care costs. On top of the expected health care inflation, last year there was a heart bypass, two hospitalizations for diabetes complications, and all those diagnostic images for new hires with dependents. George had done everything the consultants had recommended and more, and now he needed a magical solution. But all these conference gurus were still singing the same old refrain:

To reduce your company's health care costs, increase the amount employees have to pay out of their own pockets.

- Raise their copayments and deductibles.

- Limit their choice of providers and prescription drugs.

- Limit their plan options.

- Make them pay more for choice.

And a partridge in a pear tree. George wished his job was about giving employees benefits, not taking them away. Isn't that why he had chosen this field?

He glanced over at one of his fellow prisoners. Rebecca Smart, human resources director at Profitable Bank. He'd trained her as his assistant just a few years ago. She was a quick study—and look where she is now. Profitable had become the family-friendly place to work, at least in George's hometown. He sometimes thought of crawling to her for a job.

He might need to. His CEO was up in arms about that 15 percent increase, and had even accused George of inflating costs to pad his budget. George and his staff had done everything they could. Shift costs. Tighten belts. Raise copays. Raise deductibles.

The latest chart said "Raise deductibles." Hadn't he heard that somewhere before? George focused on the little red circle of light as it highlighted another percentage figure, then another, and as it slowly grew larger, undulating and finally encompassing all the data on the chart. The large blob of red light then oozed off the stage and started coming toward George. That was odd. Hoards of people were scattering and screaming….

"… and high-deductible consumer-driven health plans to…"

George shook himself awake. Oops—he hoped the people next to him hadn't noticed. He propped his eyes open, and kept on waiting for that magical solution….

Maybe health care inflation has never reminded you of *The Blob*—a low-budget 1958 horror film in which Steve McQueen battles a formless alien that consumes everyone and everything in its path, growing monstrously as it rolls along. But the comparison is not a huge stretch.

If only soaring health costs were fiction. For decades the warning has been sounded about a crisis in U.S. health care. It's been sounded so often that many employers have turned a deaf ear to it. Now, the monster is at our door. Despite our efforts to stem rising health care costs, inflation has continued to expand out of control, and corporate profits are being eaten up steadily.

Quite simply, if all the Georges in this country can't find effective ways to manage health care costs soon, their companies will lose their competitive advantage.

Or, employers will give up funding health care altogether, and the system as we know it will collapse. Imagine a world of health care where you wait in one line, and then they point you to the next line. There's a one-hour wait for one transaction—and a three-month wait for a medical procedure. You can't see the doctor you want because your name begins with the letter H. There are fewer doctors, fewer hospitals, and fewer treatment options.

Real-World Solutions

If we keep following the path we're on, those two grim realities are our only choices. What if someone told you, however, that there was another path? If you're ready for a bit of unfamiliar optimism, a glimmer of light in this murky world of health care cost containment, then read on, and open your mind to a new way of thinking about health benefits design.

Here at Pitney Bowes, we have a deep understanding of the issues confronting CEOs and their benefits managers. As the world's largest provider of mailstream hardware, software, systems and services, with more than 34,000 employees, our company has been facing the same rising health care costs everyone else has, and we've tried most of the same strategies for controlling costs. Along the way, we've discovered an entirely new approach for evaluating health care costs and designing benefits.

Some of our benefits initiatives already have been well publicized, and several major employers have followed our lead. But every CEO, CFO, and human resources and benefits managers in the United States at least should be aware of our alternative approach, because in our opinion, it's the wave of the future.

We've distilled our knowledge and experience into seven fundamental rules for achieving *total value and total return*. Whether your organization has 50 employees or 50,000, the rules in this book apply to you. They are all about shifting away from our country's obsession with health care cost containment, toward a broader focus on value-based health benefits.

Be forewarned, these rules will require a real change of perspective in the benefits department. When you understand their reasoning, however, you'll discover ways to design benefits that can make you more effective in your job, and will make a significant contribution to your organization's future health. You'll be able to impact the behavior of employees and their dependents so that they stay healthier and more productive, while at the same time you'll be controlling health care costs effectively.

Pay Me Now or Pay Me Later

To understand the solution, you must grasp the full implication of the problem.

Consider first that in the United States in 2003, we shelled out 15.3 percent of our gross domestic product to health care.[3] Compare our 15.3 percent of GDP to Germany's 10.7 percent, Canada's 9.7 percent, or France's 9.5 percent—other nations aren't saddled by costs like ours.[4] And the U.S. figure is expected to rise to 18.7 percent within 10 years.[4] If you think gasoline prices are bad, consider that employers' health insurance premiums rose by 9.2 percent between April 2004 and April 2005, a rate nearly 6 percent higher than general inflation.[5] Coverage for a family of four averaged nearly $10,880 a year, and for a single person, nearly $4,024.[5]

The Problem Is Not Getting Better, It's Getting Worse

- The baby boom generation is aging.[6] The available labor pool of Americans ages 44 to 62 will continue to increase significantly over the next few years, and at the same time the number of Americans ages 25 to 44 is projected to decrease.[6] The net result is an aging workforce with increased risks of diabetes, heart disease, and other chronic illnesses, along with all their associated costs.[2]

- Americans continue to eat high-fat, high-calorie diets, and they aren't getting enough physical activity. This further boosts the incidence of chronic disease. Already, more than 61 percent of adults age 20 to 74 are either overweight or obese.[7] In 2000, the total cost of obesity was estimated to be $117 billion.[7]

- Managed care has succeeded in shifting costs away from large health plans to other sectors of society, but employers already have wrung from it the extent of their savings, and in the meantime, managed care is failing to manage health.

- The continuing high demand for expensive new technology further increases the cost of health care.

For large, mature organizations that are paying health benefits to retirees, the problem is compounded. The health care system remains riddled with inefficiencies, and employees and their families have neither the incentive nor the knowledge to make smart decisions about their health care and lifestyle behaviors.

What It Means in Your World

How does all this gloom and doom impact you, the individual employer? For the sake of illustration, let's say your organization has 1,000 employees. If you offer them health benefits, you're probably spending about $6 million to $7.5 million per year on health care, and over the last five years those costs have probably been increasing at a rate of 10 percent to 12 percent annually—amounting to a five-year increase of 50 percent to 60 percent. Like other employers, you are facing a likely continuation of this double-digit inflation.

You've already increased employees' out-of-pocket expenses by modifying your health plans, through basic strategies such as higher deductibles and copayments. Yet even with all those changes, your $6 million expenditure is likely to increase to $8 million or $11 million within just the next three to five years. That will have a huge effect on the bottom line.

From the CEO's or CFO's perspective, your organization has to show shareholders a certain amount of return on their investments. To compensate for the shortfall from increased health care costs, one option would be to step up your sales—for a company with a 45 percent gross margin, it would need to generate approximately $1.4 million in additional sales to compensate for health care inflation. The only other obvious option would be to trim other expenses: cut jobs, reduce research and development, reduce travel and entertainment, reduce or eliminate tuition-aid programs, reduce consulting fees, limit training and development. Unfortunately, a lot of those expenses have been creating new business and a better-trained workforce for the future, so trimming them is likely to impact your organization's ability to remain competitive.

Another knee-jerk reaction by the "C-suite" and the benefits department is to continue shifting health care costs to employees or to eliminate health benefits altogether.

All of us look for short-term solutions because they help us to meet our budgets, keep our jobs, or even earn bonuses. But a Band-Aid® approach is a dangerous mistake that is likely to come back to hurt us.

Imagine all of your employees are enrolled in plans with very high deductibles and coinsurance. When they get sick, they may delay taking medications and other treatment in hopes they'll get better on their own. When it's time for a periodic cancer screening, they think first about their financial future before considering their health future. They're absent frequently from work, or they're present but unproductive because they're working around pain, fatigue, or general malaise. They're getting emergency care at the hospital for diabetes or asthma complications instead of treating themselves daily with effective maintenance medications. Some of them have given up going to the movies or dining out so they can pay their medical bills.

Chances are high that at least some of the above is already a reality in your organization, whether or not you're aware of it. You have to ask yourself: Is this the right vision for your employees, or is your benefits design driving a certain type of behavior that will negatively affect the health of both your workers and your organization?

An Opportunity in Crisis

In our ongoing dialogue with business coalitions, we're hearing that there are thousands of managers, particularly in the field of human resources, who feel isolated and helpless in managing health care costs. Maybe you are one of them. But just as an individual can emerge from the most desperate crisis as a better person, any challenge offers the opportunity to move to the forefront.

There really is hope and opportunity in the field of health benefits design. The seven rules we're providing are an alternative to the way things are being done now.

Twenty years ago, there was no such thing as a 24-hour cable news station, nor chains of gourmet coffee shops. Now 24-hour news is the norm, and there's a Starbucks on every corner. We believe the same kind of changing sea is happening now in health benefits.

Consider the seven rules as the red cones that guide a sailor to safe harbor. They are not esoteric, lofty initiatives, just smart business advice you can begin to apply right now. Achieving total value is as basic as giving your employees the benefits they want and need most, helping them to be healthier and more productive and feel good about themselves and their company, while at the same time reducing your costs. It's all about saving money, saving lives, and creating value.

The health of your organization begins with your people

GEORGE SHOOK A PACKET OF SUGAR *into his latte.*

"Hi George." He searched the coffee shop for the source of the voice.

"Rebecca! How did you survive the conference last week?"

"Quite well, actually," Rebecca said. "You mentioned you'd gone with XYZ Health Plan for your workers, right? I was thinking of calling you about getting together to discuss some new ideas, and maybe even teaming up in our health management efforts."

"That's great, but I'm sure you don't need me," George replied. "You guys at Profitable Bank are a class act all by yourselves." They had the funding, too. He'd seen the onsite fitness center under construction at the main branch. Nuts & Bolts was lucky to have an employee cafeteria.

"You have a minute to hear me out?" Rebecca asked.

"Sure, I've got a minute."

Rebecca's idea was something about "total value," about a people-centered approach to health management, about redesigning health benefits to transform a sick culture into a healthy one. Healthy culture, healthy people. It sounded logical—but somehow it didn't seem practical for George's situation. His thoughts returned to the piles of paperwork and oceans of e-mail at his office. He had costs to manage. Places to go. People to see.

"I don't mean to sound negative, but I doubt I can sell ideas like these to the CEO," George said tactfully. "Besides," he added, "when it comes to people and culture, we have nothing in common. What is there to talk about? Profitable is mostly tellers and call-center employees, right? We're all about machinists, line workers, and field sales. This isn't even apples and oranges."

"Actually, you're wrong about that. We're talking apples. People are people. And the health of any organization begins with its people."

"What do you mean?"

Rebecca has brought up the first rule you have to "get" before you can understand *total value* in health benefits. The health of your organization begins with your people.

Your people create your competitive advantage. All your products and services are a reflection of their creativity and execution. Your culture may be unique, but the basic rules of business never change: People are people. Human capital is human capital. Actually, we use the term human asset at Pitney Bowes, since we believe people are something to invest in, something that doesn't depreciate in value.

From our perspective, our company is our people. Our company is an assemblage of the human beings we depend on, who apply incredible levels of skill to inventing and maintaining the postage meters, mail-collating equipment, and machines that generate invoices for our clients. Our company is also the team of service employees who manage the mail, and the people who develop software and create business solutions. At the end of the business day, Pitney Bowes is only as good as the fellow who has to run the machinery absolutely error-free, or the delivery woman who shows up at someone's doorstep wearing our emblem on her shirt. When our people lose effectiveness, we lose customers.

Benefits managers may be unfamiliar with this language, but they need to learn it. In fact, every decision they make should be framed around this first rule. While clearly you need to keep managing health care costs, you also should know that whatever you do to invest in the health and productivity of your people is contributing in a big way to the future of your organization.

Conversely, if your benefits design supports the depletion of your human assets—if it raises barriers to effective treatment, for example, and your employees stay ill or overstressed—your business will suffer as a result. Your business may even become chronically ill. It's a vicious cycle: Business suffers because people are stressed out and sick; people get stressed out and sick because business is suffering. When stress is unrelenting and uncontrolled, it can cause minor illnesses such as backache, headache, and insomnia, and contribute to heart disease, high blood pressure, and other chronic health conditions.[8,9]

Total Value 101

How will smart benefits design reinforce your organization's health? By providing:

- **Value to your people.** A benefits structure that promotes high-level health enables people to stay committed and effective both at work and at home (see Rule 2). It increases their employability. Most people consider health in itself as their No. 1 personal asset—how often do you hear it said that someone has lost everything they own, but at least they have their health? Our own internal surveys reveal that employees value health benefits over 401K plans, vacations and holidays, pension plans, tuition aid, or any other benefits they receive. Offering good benefits addresses your employees' core values. It creates a culture in which they want to work. They become advocates of what you're trying to accomplish, and your company gains competitive advantage by attracting and retaining employees.

> **A healthy organization is:**
> - An engaged organization
> - Financially secure
> - Nimble and responsive to competitive threats and opportunities, and therefore sustainable at a high level.

- **Value to customers.** When workers are healthy, engaged, and motivated, guess what? Everyone from line workers to sales associates, customer service reps and supervisors are more likely to be working at top form. This means they are producing high-quality products and services. This creates value for your customers.

- **Value to shareholders.** When customers value the company's products and services, your organization will experience increased sales and profits as a result. Healthier profits create value for your organization's investors.

Happy employees lead to happy customers, which leads to happy investors. And the healthier the investments are, the more nimble and responsive your organization is to competitive threats and opportunities, and the more sustainable it is at a high level. Instead of a negative cycle of chronic illness, a positive cycle is set in motion: Shareholders invest robustly, so the organization is able to continue investing in its people, products, and services. Customers remain satisfied; employees continually feel empowered by the fruits of their labor. Each facet of the triad nourishes the others.

The important point here is that whether your organization is sick or healthy, *your people* are what sets the cycle in motion. Everything begins with your people. Healthy people are key to a healthy organization. Therefore, health should be a key corporate value.

Supporting Health as a Core Value

Don't miss that last statement; it's an important one. *Health should be a key corporate value.* By managing the health of your people—your most strategic asset— you are bringing value to customers and shareholders and enhancing your organization's competitive advantage and its long-term sustainability.

We're not alone in saying this. A growing number of U.S. employers already are supporting health as a core value. For example:

- **Aetna Inc.'s** own research has shown measurable improvements in work productivity among employees who improved their health risks.[10] The company provides incentives for designated preventive care services, along with an online healthy-lifestyle program, weight management programs, fitness centers, a 24-hour information line with access to a registered nurse, and other offerings.[11]

- **Bank One,** based in Chicago, has provided leading-edge programs to its employees in such areas as primary prevention, wellness, prenatal education, and disease management. In addition, it has been a leader in studying and reporting the relationships between health risks, disease, and productivity measures such as presenteeism.[12-17]

- **DaimlerChrysler** has been recognized as one of the leading companies in corporate health practices. Their occupational health and safety programs have successfully integrated health and safety initiatives throughout the organization—through injury prevention, wellness programming, and medical and disability management.[18]

- **The Dow Chemical Company** provides a comprehensive and integrated health management initiative that is designed to build a "culture of health." Their health strategy links key company functions to "ensure a synergistic and maximally effective effort to support health and financial outcomes for the benefit of employees, their families, and Dow's stakeholders."[19,20]

- **HighSmith Inc.** provides a first-class work environment for its 220 employees—based on its T.A.G. initiative:"**T**otal commitment to developing human potential; **A**ccess to learning opportunities; and **G**rowth as an individual and as a company." As such, its wellness programs and related services are designed to help create an environment in which employee's decisions support their own development and the company's business goals.[21]

- **Intel Corporation** is developing and implementing an integrated approach to employee health and productivity management through its "3-R Strategy—redesign of benefits, reduction of risks, and reform of IT." An integral goal of this strategy is to "actively engage employees with their benefits." As such, benefits design that includes incentives is intended to help leverage employee decisions and actions regarding personal health risks.[22]

- **Quad/Graphics** embraces the value that their employees are the company's greatest asset and health care is an investment in protecting their workforce. The company has developed a comprehensive approach to health and safety that includes a health information system, inhouse medical and rehabilitation clinics, wellness programming, and a benefits plan design that provides full coverage for routine health exams.[18]

- **Union Pacific Corporation's** award-winning Health Track program is viewed as an integral part of its business strategy. The program includes health risk assessments, vocational rehabilitation, company-sponsored fitness facilities, train cars converted into fitness facilities, multisite health risk intervention programming, medical consumer education, alertness management initiatives, and medical surveillance programs.[23]

These companies acknowledge, from the top down, that an organization with a culture that supports employee health has a greater chance of staying competitive. The bottom line? How your own organization designs its employee health benefits can support—or possibly undermine—the short- and long-term health of your organization.

2

To realize total value, you must understand total costs

GEORGE SUDDENLY remembered his latte, but it had grown cold. He ordered two more, one for Rebecca. The hum of coffee-shop conversation made a pleasant white noise in the background.

"Okay, I get it," he replied. "Health is a core value. And it all begins with our people. I can see how that's true at Nuts & Bolts. Right now our sales manager is out for back surgery, and without him, I'll bet you anything sales quotas aren't being met. When my assistant had the flu last winter, I fell behind in my own work. Everything came to a standstill. I'm still repairing some of the mistakes the temp made.

"But Rebecca, all this healthy employee stuff—isn't it a lofty ideal? I mean, show me the money. As it is," he continued, "my job in the benefits department is to deal with the line item of health care costs, not to increase productivity. Productivity is the realm of supervisors, or human resources, or the CEO. I have to show results in managing health costs or I'm not doing the job the big boss expects. You remember how it was when you were with us. There's no time for anything extra!"

"Direct health care costs are huge," Rebecca agreed. "We all need to manage health costs. But would you believe that direct costs may be only 30 percent to 50 percent of the total cost of poor health at Nuts & Bolts?"

That one didn't sound so believable.

"You can't manage what you don't measure," Rebecca continued. "If you're measuring only one-half to one-third of what actually exists, you're not truly managing the full cost burden of ill *health. Suppose you answered the phone tomorrow, and it was your CFO saying, 'I need some figures on the total cost of health care by 10 o'clock to present to the president. What is the cost including disability and workers' compensation?'"*

"I doubt he'd do that," George muttered. "He never has before."

"How about a year or two from now? Chances are he will be asking by then. What will you say when he does?"

For decades now, employers and health plans have been measuring direct health care costs according to the traditional dashboard metrics of inpatient and outpatient costs, doctors' fees, laboratory and diagnostic expenses, and pharmaceutical costs.

However, there's a solid body of research showing that indirect costs, such as absenteeism, short-term disability, and workers' compensation, also contribute significantly to the impact of total health costs.[14,20,24,25,26] We're also beginning to see data showing that sick people produce sick work—errors, poor quality, accidents, and lower output.[13,16] This loss of productivity on the job is known as presenteeism. Together, all these indirect costs may comprise up to two-thirds of the total cost burden of employee health to employers.[20,25] Many employers are beginning to factor them strategically into the health cost equation.

Do you want to make yourself truly indispensable to your organization? Learn the true cost of poor health. That's when you can really start managing costs. Rule 2: To realize total value in health benefits design, you have to understand total costs.

Pitney Bowes knows all its direct and indirect health care costs, because the CFO, president, or chairman calls the benefits department frequently to ask what they are. A number of savvy CEOs at other companies are asking the same question. Knowing the answer allows our company to design highly targeted, creative interventions tailored to high-cost areas so we can get the strongest possible return from our efforts.

Our CEO, Mike Critelli, believes our strategic cost-saving interventions strengthen the company's position in the marketplace. For example: Pitney Bowes competes in the outsourcing business—all else being equal with our competitors, every ounce of value Pitney Bowes can squeeze from higher productivity, and every dollar of expense it can trim by lowering the cost of health care, absenteeism, and short- and long-term disability, can help give us the competitive edge. Our CEO sees another advantage: Knowing the total costs increases the predictability of Pitney Bowes' expenses and thus the predictability of its net income, which increases the multiple on the company's stock.

For example, in one large study, researchers found that average absence and disability losses were 29 percent of total dollars for physical health conditions and 47 percent for all mental health conditions.[27] This is a huge margin of error when assessing the organization's true cost burden and does not take into account the impact of on-the-job productivity loss—presenteeism.

The bottom line: After factoring in the indirect costs, you may see fit to re-engineer the entire focus of your health management strategy, including benefits plan design, health promotion programs, disease management programs, related incentives, and environmental improvements to address your leading *total* cost drivers.

The True Cost of Headache or Flu

You need to mine data from your own population, because every employee population is different, even within separate facilities of the same company. In the meantime, the argument for doing so is supported by a wealth of existing research pointing to the potential total cost of certain health conditions. For example:

- **Irritable bowel syndrome.** Some 10 percent to 20 percent of adults suffer from this often debilitating gastrointestinal disorder.[28] In one study, researchers found that workers with IBS miss nearly three times as many workdays—13.4

days per year compared to 4.9—as employees without IBS symptoms.[28] At Comerica, a large banking organization, employees with IBS reported a 15 percent loss in productivity when compared to employees without IBS symptoms.[29] Cost modeling predicted that every $1 spent on IBS medication therapy could save the company $3.75 in avoided productivity losses.[30]

- **Allergies.** Allergies affect as many as 40 to 50 million Americans.[31] Employees with severe allergy symptoms are absent 1.67 times more often and have three times as many injuries as healthy employees, according to a study of manufacturing workers.[32] Symptoms during prime pollen season are associated with a 10 percent increase in presenteeism in workers who are not on effective medication.[12]

- **Asthma.** Some 31.3 million Americans have been diagnosed with asthma in their lifetime, according to a 2001 estimate, and cases are on the rise.[33] Asthma sufferers have reported an average of three days of work impairment within a 30-day period, according to one study.[34]

- **Depression.** Depressed workers have 1.5 to 3.2 more short-term disability days per month research shows.[35] Employees with major depression experience an average of 4.3 days of work impairment within 30 days.[34]

- **Diabetes.** About 7 percent of the U.S. population has diabetes.[36] There were 1.5 million new cases of diabetes in people 20 years or older in 2005.[36] In a 2002 study, men with diabetes lost 3.1 more workdays per year than men without diabetes, and women with diabetes lost 0.6 more workdays than women without diabetes.[37]

- **Influenza.** Each year 10 percent to 20 percent of Americans come down with the flu.[38] A case of flu leads to 2.8 days lost from work, an average per-episode cost to the employer of $398 per person in lost work time.[38] Flu-vaccination programs for adults younger than 65 have been linked to a 34 percent to 44 percent reduction in physician visits, and a 32 percent to 45 percent decrease in lost workdays.[39]

- **Migraine.** Approximately 18 percent of females and 6 percent of males suffer from migraines.[40] Symptoms of migraine headache lead to 3.2 lost workdays per year in absenteeism and 4.9 lost workday equivalents in presenteeism, research indicates.[16] Bank One concludes that migraine symptoms cost the company at least $21.5 million per year in absenteeism and $24.4 million in presenteeism.[16]

- **Mulitple conditions.** One study found that when a mental disorder such as depression was present with either hypertension, arthritis, asthma, or ulcers (comorbid conditions) the greater the probability of job impairment (presenteeism).[41]

Assessing Your Own Total Costs

The ease with which you can obtain your own company-specific data may depend on your organization's size and available resources. Simply put, you'll want to obtain cost data broken down according to each of the disease and injury burdens affecting your organization.

- **Your health plan** can provide a breakdown of both inpatient and outpatient direct medical costs. The most recent claims data can be compared with previous years' numbers to show where the costs are increasing most dramatically. Ask for a projected estimate of next year's costs, as well.

- **Your workers' compensation carrier** can similarly cost out the specific safety incidents your people are experiencing.

- **Your disability insurance company** can tell you which groups of employees are out on short-term disability, for how long, for which diseases, and at what cost.

- **Your payroll department** can provide absenteeism data for hourly employees. Collecting these data for salaried employees may be more difficult, but it can be done if the appropriate tracking systems are in place.

Proceed carefully, taking appropriate measures to ensure the confidentiality of your employees' health data at each step in your process. There are several practical, low-cost avenues to integrating your siloed information that thoroughly protect your employees' privacy.

By compiling and integrating all this information broken down by disease, you now can take a proactive, person-centric approach to cost analysis—bringing the focus back to your people. This is the beginning of value-based health care decision making.[26]

Making sense of the data can be as simple as creating a spreadsheet. List your grand total of direct health care costs, followed by your totals for disability, workers' compensation, etc. Let's say your company is spending $5 million total on direct health care costs, $1.5 million for worker's compensation, and $0.5 million for short-term disability; that gives you $7 million in total health-related costs. Now, place that $7 million expense in the numerator and your company's revenues of $100 million in the denominator—that's how the CFO will look at it—and you'll discover that poor health is costing your organization more than a pretty penny.

Next, plug in the estimates of next year's costs from your health care plan, your workers' compensation carrier, and your short-term disability carrier; you may see, for example, that total costs are due to increase by $1.2 million. The question becomes, how will that higher figure impact your organization's profitability for next year? If the company can absorb the additional cost, that's fine, but most companies can't.

Once you've entered the summary data, you can begin to look closely at the major drivers of cost—whether they are cancer, maternity, asthma, diabetes, or heart attacks.

For example, within five specific disease groups, you may see two with costs increasing at double-digit or high single-digit rates—that's where you can consider putting in place plan designs to help to manage those costs.

Costing out presenteeism. Quantifying presenteeism is an evolving science, and thus may be more of a challenge. If you can't measure presenteeism, at least have knowledge of it, because for sure it's impacting your organization.[24,25]

Presenteeism is all about your people who come to work, but are not fully engaged in their work because of a health or personal problem. They spend time around the water cooler talking about their aches and pains. They shuffle papers or tap at their keyboard to give a false impression they're focused on work. They may give substandard service to customers, or neglect to insert key data in a report, or they are mentally or physically slow, making them a safety risk. They're being paid a full day's pay for a full day's work, but they may be *working only at two-thirds their capacity.*[20]

Let's say you have a project engineering team with five developers, and one of them has seasonal asthma during the crucial spring and fall work periods. During those seasons the other team members will have to pick up the slack, which brings additional stress to them. If the person has a prolonged absence, you'll have to bring in a temporary replacement or an outside consultant, which places an extra cost burden on the company.

Psychosocial issues, such as financial troubles, addiction, caregiving difficulties, or family problems, also can contribute in a big way to productivity losses.

Presenteeism is more difficult to quantify within the indirect workforce, such as distribution, logistics, warehousing, or administrative staff; and easier to quantify in direct operations where work tasks may lend themselves to more objective measurement. For example, one may be able to measure[24]:

- work output

- number and magnitude of errors

- injury rates

- time spent off task

- ability to perform at peak level

The majority of studies conducted so far are based on decrements of work performance. A classic example is the pioneering research of Chicago-based Bank One that studied the influence of health risks and illness on the productivity of call-center employees. The company looked at measures, such as call rates, on-hold time, and failure to meet a productivity goal, and compared them to data related to illness, health risks, absences, and so on. The findings? They found a significant inverse relationship between productivity measures and health risks and certain health problems.[13]

In coming years, presenteeism will play a greater role in total cost assessment, particularly as researchers agree increasingly on how to define and measure it. For the time being, there are a number of self-reporting presenteeism instruments available that have demonstrated scientific rigor.[24] Or, simply canvas your population to get a sense of the impact and causes of presenteeism. Pitney Bowes did a telephone survey a few years ago and asked people what was keeping them from contributing to their work. They told us about their pain, their sniffles, and their family issues. Someone would say, "I can't think clearly because I have a head cold."

More sophisticated analysis. If your organization is large enough and you have adequate resources, consider using an integrated database to perform a refined analysis of your total costs and high-cost health conditions. Current information management technology allows you to collect transaction information from diverse information systems such as disability, worker's compensation, absenteeism, and so forth, and perform a more efficient and sophisticated analysis of cost and usage patterns. This allows you to target your opportunities for change more effectively.

Additionally, Pitney Bowes relies heavily on predictive modeling. This sophisticated tool allows us to take a highly proactive approach in which we anticipate future costs rather than relying solely on cost history. Predictive modeling takes into account population demographics such as age, gender, and income level, so we can compare prevalent diseases at a specific company location to public health benchmarks for that region. What we learn enables us to intervene early with high-cost health conditions— and that only adds to our competitive edge.

Not Rocket Science

Some CEOs can't get their hands around the concept of indirect health care costs; they think: If people get sick they'll catch up later, so we'll just keep paying their salaries and leave it at that. But our CEO understands. He used to be in human resources; he's seen firsthand the impact of poor health on productivity and short- and long-term disability. And the good news, he reports, is that other CEOs are beginning to understand this "new math" and are acting upon it as well.

Nothing Pitney Bowes has done related to health care, health promotion, or health benefits is rocket science. In the end, it comes down to good old common sense backed up by a tremendous amount of data. A friend once said, "If you can't trust the people who made the box, think outside of the box." In the absence of conclusive data supporting a clear argument for investing in interventions, rely on common sense and think through to logical conclusions.

For example, Pitney Bowes made a decision a few years back to invest in onsite primary care clinics at our major facilities in Connecticut, Wisconsin, Washington, and Maryland. At that time, most other corporations had eliminated worksite clinics entirely, and the consultants warned us it would be a terrible waste of our money—"Where's the evidence?" they asked us. For us, however, the clinics made complete sense. Every time our employees sought primary care treatment outside the workplace they lost work time and incurred much higher costs. Our own clinics would be able to deliver the care for 60 cents on the dollar, plus they would trim lost work time significantly. We didn't need to work up a full business case to see the logic in that.

The point is, if you are to maintain a position of value in your organization, you have to be proactive and create solutions. Remember Rule 1? The health of your organization begins with your people. You have to think about how you can have employees performing at their best every day because the health of your company depends on it.

If you internalize anything at all about Rule 2, it's that direct medical costs are only the tip of the iceberg. "Health and productivity are inextricably linked" in their contributions to total health care costs.[24] If you really believe in achieving total value—in finding value in all aspects of health and productivity—then you will want to provide the health benefits and other support services that address all the costs of ill health.

Higher costs don't always mean higher value

"SORRY ABOUT THE TEEN-AGE CLUTTER," *Rebecca said as she slipped the car into drive. "This is my son's car. Mine is in the shop."*

She had picked up George at his workplace to ferry them to their lunch meeting—an opportunity to build on last week's discussion. George was intrigued to learn more. Already, he realized, his job horizons had been expanded.

"I was thinking of a local eatery, but how about Profitable's onsite cafeteria, our treat?" Rebecca asked. "This way you can see a bit of the bank behind the scenes."

"Sounds great," George replied.

The car pulled out smoothly, hugging the road.

"I can't believe that little guy of yours is already driving," he remarked, adding: "You chose a good car for a teenager. This make has a top safety rating, doesn't it?"

"I convinced him that for starting college this fall, he needs a safe, dependable vehicle that won't need constant repairs and put him in the poorhouse," Rebecca said. "It has a few years on it, but it runs like a dream. It has driver's side air bags, gets decent mileage, and these engines run forever. We got it for just $4,500, with a three-month warranty. It took some negotiating."

"That's a real value. I'll have to start thinking about these things in a few years for my own son," George added. "You have to shop carefully when safety is in the balance."

"It is all about value," Rebecca said. "You don't mind my talking about it on the ride over, do you?"

"That's the topic," George remarked.

"It's funny," she continued. "Few people would dream of spending even a couple thousand dollars on a car without knowing they were getting good quality in return. But look at what employers do. We're the global business leaders. Yet, when it comes to health benefits, we are constantly making million-dollar decisions regarding services that have limited measurements for quality or outcome, and no warranty.

"That's the world of employer-funded health care for you, I guess," George said with a chuckle. But Rebecca wasn't smiling.

"Imagine when George Jr. goes off to college," Rebecca went on, "you buy a pricey car for him with no warranty, and you know nothing about its gas mileage, its safety ratings, or even its track record. You don't bother to have it checked out beforehand by your mechanic. Imagine that's how everyone else is buying their cars. Higher costs don't always mean higher value—you'd probably end up with a real lemon. An exorbitant lemon with a sunroof, a global positioning system, and a built-in voice that tells you when the door is ajar.

"That's just what we're doing with health care," she continued. "Employees are demanding all the latest high-tech treatments, and we're paying for them. But there's no consistent system in place to measure quality. Did you know that physicians deliver only 50 percent of services recommended in evidence-based guidelines?"

George wasn't even sure what that meant.

"Suppose half of all the services you got from your local auto mechanic were not the optimal repairs recommended by the dealer," Rebecca explained. "Think about it. Health should be a key corporate value. Yet, we engage in exactly these kinds of flawed purchasing decisions when managing the health of our people."

Clearly, we U.S. employers have purchased a high-ticket luxury vehicle for our employees. Health care in this country today is a $2 trillion industry.[3] And health care spending continues to outpace general inflation and salary increases significantly. For example, since 2000, health premiums have increased 73 percent.[5]

Our country spends more on health care than other industrialized nations do, but does high cost necessarily mean high value?[42] Definitely not.

- Many other Western countries are paying significantly less per capita on health care than we are—even as they are providing care for all their citizens.[42]

- We have some 45 million uninsured in this country, and among industrialized nations,[1] we rank in the bottom quartile for life expectancy and infant mortality.[43]

- When compared to Australia, Canada, New Zealand, Britain, and Germany, the United States is an outlier in such health indexes as medical error rates, inefficient care, and high access and cost barriers.[44]

- Racial and ethnic minorities in the U.S. tend to receive lower quality medical care, regardless of insurance status and income.[45]

- Many experts agree that the U.S. health care system is riddled with waste, duplication, errors, and inefficiencies.[46]

Our country became a global economic leader through its business savvy. Now, if we can just direct that same savvy toward value-based health care purchasing, we have the power to start turning this health crisis around.

If demanding high value in health care seems a formidable task for a lone employer, read on. There are actually some very simple things you can do on a local level to help transform the quality of care available to your employees and their dependents. It mainly has to do with benefits design, incentives, employee education, and teamwork with your health plan and with other employers.

Quality Solutions

Low cost + high quality = high value. Here are some ways to make this equation work for your organization and its employees:

Problem: misaligned incentives. Health care providers continually receive incentives to provide low-cost care with no consideration for quality. Commonly, the end result is lower quality and higher costs. How can this be? Think back to Rebecca's car-repair analogy: Imagine you promise all your car-repair business to a local service station based not on appropriate, results-oriented service, but only on how low their hourly rates are and how speedy their mechanics are. You know what kind of service you're apt to get: plenty of speedy, lower-cost repairs on your car, including repairs you never really needed and repairs to mend all the previously botched repairs. Because the incentive you offer is not aligned with your priorities of quality and value, your car stays in the shop, and your repair bills soar.

It's similar when you promise all your business to the health care providers who deliver speedy, low-cost treatment. Without quality in the equation, your employees face an increased risk of unnecessary procedures, complications, and other adverse outcomes. The procedures patients really should be receiving may go neglected, including preventive care and chronic disease management. No matter how well-intentioned health care providers are, if they are not held accountable for ensuring that patients with diabetes, for example, adhere to the A1c test to measure blood glucose levels, your employees' diabetes could easily go uncontrolled. Uncontrolled diabetes can cost you upwards of $20,000 per employee per year, compared to a cost of $1,500 for well-managed diabetes.

Solution: Design health benefits to reward high quality. If you're ever going to arrive at total value, you have to believe in pay for performance, because this is the ultimate solution to quality of care. Pay for performance is all about finding the doctors and hospitals that provide the best care and the most efficient use of resources—that is, the best overall value—and then driving your patients to them through plan design.

Talk with your health plan, and with other employers served by the same plan, about strategies such as tiered reimbursement, in which plan members have to pay more for the option of visiting higher-cost, lower-quality providers. If you do this, you will find your efforts will move the entire marketplace toward a higher quality level, since providers will want the associated recognition and financial rewards.

Pay for performance ultimately holds medical providers accountable for the power of the pen. They will be more likely to frame their prescribed treatments around evidenced-based standards. We predict that over time as more and more employers move toward pay for performance, physician and hospital networks will become obsolete.

Another way to reward high quality is to design benefits that increase employees' access to "centers of excellence." Providers at top-performing cancer centers, for example, do higher volumes of specialized procedures and thus tend to meet higher outcome standards.

Medical providers also can be given direct incentives to offer higher quality care. The Bridges to Excellence program is an example (see www.bridgestoexcellence.org).[47] Under this program, physicians who adhere to certain treatment standards for diabetes or cardiac care, or whose office systems use efficient systematic processes, receive bonus payments from employers that can increase their income by up to 10 percent. High-performing physicians are additionally recognized by their inclusion in provider directories. Bridges to Excellence is administered by the National Committee for Quality Assurance (NCQA) and Medstat; employers include such organizations as UPS, General Electric, and Ford Motor Company.

Problem: Lack of a consistent system to measure quality. Many health policy experts agree that our existing health care system is built and incentivized on the delivery of services with limited accountability to demonstrate value.[46] Like automobile chop shops, different providers tend to treat the same health problem in different ways. Quality guidelines are not established universally, and those that are, generally are not enforced. According to one national study, Americans receive only about one-half of recommended medical care processes for diabetes, asthma, congestive heart failure, and other conditions.[48]

In addition, patients often are seeing multiple doctors and receiving multiple prescriptions and multiple tests; and because the system is so highly matrixed, employers have no way to control the costs or determine the quality of care received. No universal, computerized system for medical records exists. Even in this age of information, if specialists want to access their patients' hospital records, they often have to make physical visits to the hospitals and decipher a handwritten chart.

Solution: Agree on standards and information systems that will apply to all providers. As in the Bridges to Excellence program, all medical care providers should be encouraged to adhere to evidence-based treatment. At the same time, we should be introducing real accountability in the health care system for the actual health of the individual. Today's incentives are all based on episodic or one-time incidents. To gauge quality more effectively, we should be asking patients questions such as: "Has your physician called you in the last six months just to ask you how you are?" "If your doctor did call you, did he or she ask whether you've been doing blood-sugar testing for your diabetes?" "Are you receiving blood pressure checks?" "Are you taking medications—and if not, why not?" If doctors are not following established practices for disease management, it may be because they are reimbursed by the health plan only for sick care. Incentives need to be realigned toward preventive maintenance, not just repairs.

You can help to achieve consistent standards in your community by participating in quality initiatives through your local health care coalition. Talk with your health plan about quality initiatives; ask local hospitals how they measure and document quality, whether through NCQA or Health Plan Employer Data and Information Set (HEDIS) standards. Work with these groups to develop and promote "provider report cards" on which health plans and hospitals are rated according to established benchmarks of quality (e.g., the standards set forth by the Washington, D.C.-based Leapfrog Group).[49] Then, drive adherence through incentives built into your benefits design. Many health care coalitions already have on hand a series of tools for measuring quality.

The key is, even a small- to mid-size employer may have more leverage in its local marketplace than it realizes. A study of our own workforce found that a mere handful of physicians served many of our Connecticut employees. Due to word-of-mouth referral, it's likely most of your employees in one locale are seeing the same 2 percent to 3 percent of local physicians, and frequenting just one local hospital.

Have you ever brought up the topic of quality with other employers in your community? Typically, the answer is no, simply because employers feel they are too busy, or that their issues are unique, or that they don't know the right questions to ask. A few years ago Pitney Bowes didn't know the right questions, but now we do.

Problem: Patients are demanding inappropriate or higher-cost services. When your employees visit their doctors, chances are they'll leave with prescriptions, X-rays, or some other tangible evidence that they got their money's worth. Doctors comply with requests for these services because they want repeat business. They'll prescribe an antibiotic for a viral infection knowing full well the drug works only on bacterial infections. And they'll be happy to offer the latest tests—if only because they don't want to be held liable should the person's health go astray.

Solution: Educate employees. Drive quality by encouraging employees to adhere to effective, appropriate treatment. Teach them what kind of care they should seek—for example, appropriate preventive screenings according to their ages and other health risks—and what kind of care is unnecessary. Give them resources to support their medical self-care decisions. Give them more personal accountability for their health. For more about these strategies, see Rule 4.

Problem: The health plan is denying claims for effective treatment. Even in the best-designed benefits plan, glitches can occur during the review process resulting in denial of essential treatment.

Solution: Participate in the appeals process. At Pitney Bowes, we handle the appeals process for second- and third-level denials of claims. We tell employees, if your claim is denied and you fail at the first level of appeal, come to us, not to the health plan. Employees can file appeals with our benefits administration committee. Not only does this process help the employee to access critical health care, it also serves as a window into quality management for us. This is another example of how we can get to know our employees, their needs, and their environment, so we can modify programs, policies and benefits designs accordingly.

According to Johnna Torsone, our senior vice president and chief human resources officer, "The challenge (CEO) Mike Critelli has laid out to us in the last 12 to 13 years is that he expects us to provide higher quality to our employees, and at the same time show improvement from a cost perspective. Many people would consider that to be paradoxical. But all it requires is some critical thinking."

Whether you are teaming up with other employers to change the marketplace or intervening with health care claims on a case-by-case basis, it's all about promoting quality of care. Quality is key to value-based medicine. Simply put, the largest service sector of our economy has limited accountability for demonstrating need, quality, and outcomes. To achieve quality, employers, employees, and health plans must all work together in a consistent manner.

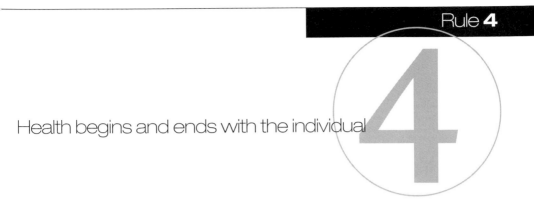

Health begins and ends with the individual

THE WORD QUALITY *echoed in George's mind as he walked through the parking lot toward the bank's main entrance, hot on Rebecca's heels. A balding gentleman in a T-shirt and sweatpants brushed past him.*

"Excuse me! I have to get my 10K today!" the man explained congenially over his shoulder as he walked past briskly, arms pumping. A memorable character. A man of quality. George caught up to Rebecca and gestured toward the speed-walker before the man rounded the corner.

"Fitness fanatics are everywhere," he mused.

"Who? Oh, that's Jerry Worthy."

Jerry Worthy? The name had a familiar ring.

Rebecca ushered George into the lobby—an imposing marble-bedecked entryway, suitable for the central offices of a flourishing regional bank.

"Hi, Rebecca," a woman said with a beaming smile. This place had a highly professional polish, just like Rebecca; yet there was something about it that made George feel uplifted and energized. Most financial institutions made him feel diminutive, if not slightly depressed.

They took a detour down a side hall, and Rebecca punched the elevator call button. A sign by the elevator stated, "Take the Stairs Instead." Before he could think about it, he watched as one bank employee, then another, scooted into the stairwell. He and Rebecca chose the elevator.

As the doors slid open again, colorful posters were lining the walls: An onsite health fair next month; reminder to wash your hands to prevent the flu; a lunch talk today by a local nutritionist.

"This is a health club," George remarked. He was experiencing a kind of culture shock here, but at the same time he was already feeling very much at home. He certainly could work at this place.

"Grab a tray," Rebecca said as they entered the bustling cafeteria. "You should try the broiled fish and fresh vegetables. Not just because they're less expensive than the burgers and fries, they do an appetizing job with healthy food here." The two flowed through the line to the cash register and soon sat across from each other at a table.

"The bank subsidizes the healthier food selections," Rebecca explained. "That's why the baked potato chips cost less than the fried chips, and the fish less than the burgers." George tried an offered chip.

"I wanted you to see how things are done here," she announced. "We want employees to take charge of their health, and people who come into our facility get that message within the first half-hour of walking around. We aim to create a culture of health. You see, health begins and ends with the individual. Achieving total value depends on increasing the personal accountability of your employees and empowering them to make the right decisions about their health. Of course, the message really comes through loud and clear when it comes from Jerry Worthy, our chairman and CEO."

That's where George had heard that name.

Some years ago one of Pitney Bowes' employees decided to retire after many years with the company. He was the nicest guy you could want to be around, gentle and caring. Within months of retirement he suffered a massive, fatal heart attack. An immediate thought arose: This man was too young and too nice to die. The next thought was, why hadn't his condition been prevented or treated earlier? The answer was that he hadn't been adhering to regular doctor's visits and he hadn't been adhering to heart medications or a healthy lifestyle. He left behind a wife, children, and grandchildren, and an empty space in everyone's life. That was a defining moment for us. We realized, among other things, that our health management initiatives needed a stronger emphasis on the individual.

A major reason for out-of-control health care costs and related productivity losses is that individuals ultimately do not take responsibility for their own health. They may feel they have no control over their smoking or eating habits; or they already feel over-burdened by responsibilities; or they believe they are immune to chronic illness; or they "forget" to take their medication(s). For example:

- Adherence to treatment regimens for chronic health conditions averages 50 percent.[50]

- 51 percent of hypertensive patients adhere to recommended treatment.[50]

- Less than 2 percent of adults with diabetes adhere to recommended standards of care.[50]

- In cases of severe asthma, optimal control of symptoms would produce savings of approximately 45 percent of direct medical costs.[50]

- Modifiable lifestyle behaviors account for 90 percent of adult-onset diabetes cases, 80 percent of coronary heart disease cases, and 70 percent of stroke and colon cancer cases.[51]

Lifestyle and self-responsibility are the most significant factors influencing health, experts believe. Individuals have more influence on their health through lifestyle than the medical system, their environment, or family histories.[52] Yet amazingly, the U.S. health system is not set up to empower individuals to take charge of their own health. It's devoted to rescuing—with heart surgery, for example, or with cardiac rehabilitation. Often the rescue comes at great expense, or worse, it comes too late.

In the previous chapter, we discussed quality of care and its critical role in achieving total value in health benefits. So, how do you drive quality on the employee end?

Through adherence. You can have the best health plan in the world, you can have the best health promotion programs in the country, you can have all the top hospitals and doctors delivering evidence-based medicine to your people, but if the employee doesn't take her blood pressure medication as prescribed or participate in your weight management program, then all your other investments in quality may be for naught.

The health of your organization begins with your people—that's Rule 1. Rule 4 peels away a layer from the first rule to reveal that everything about your people's health goes back to the level of the individual. *Employee health begins and ends with the employee.*

To empower employees at Pitney Bowes, we start out with the basic premise that it's our responsibility to create a culture that values health. We provide education, benefits, programs, incentives, and policies that support that value. We offer healthy food choices, alternatives for physical activity, a nonsmoking environment, free onsite clinics at our major employee locations, disease management programs, and preventive services; and we ensure that everything is highly accessible to the employee. We communicate the message about health, from the top down, through both word and action.

Very purposefully missing from the statement above is a suggestion that we also "manage the health of the employee." It's up to employees and their family members to manage their own health. We can empower people to engage by offering supports, but we can't force them to engage.

Lessons From Financial Planning

Key to employee empowerment is a cultural shift that moves employees' perceptions from one of *benefits entitlement* to that of *shared ownership* in personal and organizational health. Any employer can help create that shift with the proper tools.

You can find some encouragement in the fact that the financial planning industry already has effected a similar shift. Back in 1992, when Jack Mahoney was working for a large consulting firm, the firm surveyed a group of employees about their fears, wishes and desires. The survey revealed that people had two major goals. One was: *I want to retire with wealth.* The second was: *I want to retire with health.* The consultants explored the connection between those two statements, and noticed that achieving either goal requires people to begin taking personal responsibility for their actions at the earliest age possible. How much you invest today in a 401K plan or other savings vehicle will determine your future wealth. How much you exercise today, or how well you adhere to your daily blood pressure medication, can impact your future health.

One might say that health care today is where financial planning was 15 years ago. Through strategic 401K plan design and educational efforts, many people are finding that they need to be more accountable for their financial security and change their saving and spending behaviors accordingly. In the process, they have discovered that as they accumulate financial assets, they gain a greater sense of control and well-being. They experience that they now have something in place for themselves and their family members, something that continues to grow in value through their personal contributions. That's empowerment.

Today, investing in a 401K plan is relatively simple: You put aside 5 percent to 10 percent of your pay, and watch the savings build. However, today if you're diagnosed with diabetes, you probably don't know where to invest your self-management efforts. Your choices are complex and the treatment message is unclear. Your doctor may give you a 5-minute dissertation filled with esoteric terms, while the Internet may offer you reams of information irrelevant to your situation.

What brought about behavior change surrounding 401K plans? The industry identified the barriers to saving for retirement, created programs to address the barriers, and engaged the federal government and other agencies to highlight the issue so people would be getting the word from multiple sources. In health care, we're likely to go the same way. The barriers may seem formidable, but they can be overcome. See the action steps below.

Designing for Personal Accountability

To take the analogy further, we can look at the shift from defined contribution benefits plans to 401Ks as being like today's shift from standard managed care plans to the new high-deductible, consumer-driven health plans. Back in the 1970s and '80s, employers began to get out of the business of pension plans because they were expensive, highly regulated by the federal government, and burdensome to manage. Many of them started enrolling their people automatically in 401K plans with a positive opt-out to create forced savings. Now we're entering the same moment in time for health care. Led by small- to mid-size companies, growing numbers of employers are getting out of the health care business, and/or looking seriously at high-deductible plans that shift more responsibility to individuals.

With these plans, coverage kicks in after at least a $1,100 deductible (for individuals) or $2,200 per family, typically paying 80 percent to 90 percent of health care expenses. After $5,000 of total out-of-pocket payouts in a given year (individual) or $10,000 per family, the plans are required by law to pay 100 percent of remaining expenses.[53] Meanwhile, the employee can make additional pretax deposits to a savings or investment account for use toward future medical expenses. This savings component combined with the risk of high out-of-pocket expenses requires the consumer to assume a similar sense of responsibility a 401K plan does in terms of managing funds, anticipating future expenditures, and making wise use of services—skills that are key to personal accountability in health care consumerism.

High-deductible health plans promise significantly lower premiums, particularly for small- to midsize employers based on their underwriting and experience levels. And these plans do have value for specific employee populations. But keep in mind that if they are the only choice you offer to employees, they are not likely to empower. Quite the contrary. Imagine how you'd feel if your homeowner's insurance broker suddenly announced he was moving you from your current $250 deductible and $2,000 out-of-pocket maximum for damages to a $5,000 deductible with a $20,000 out-of-pocket maximum. You'd probably feel angry at being manipulated—if the roof blew off your house, you'd have to go into debt to replace it. In many cases, an employee is willing to pay more up front for the peace of mind that comes with lower financial risk.

Whether someone makes $20,000 a year or $100,000, people actually are pretty smart when it comes to their own health care, as long as they are given the right information translated in a way that lets them make informed decisions. Basically, if you want people to behave like adults, you've got to treat them like adults—adults you will educate and empower. You let them make a set of decisions, but you don't set up a series of roadblocks for them. You give them high-quality, cost-efficient choices where it counts, and you respect them as adults.

Steps Toward Empowerment

How do you drive, enforce, and incentivize personal accountability throughout your organization? Here are a few simple, doable action steps to help empower your population:

- Begin with a clear understanding of your culture, its needs and interests, so you can tailor your strategy for high impact.

- Continually reinforce this message to employees: "You matter. Your health is important to you and to us. You're accountable."

- Teach employees how to be wise medical care consumers: how to choose a doctor, adhere to prescribed treatments, navigate their health benefits plan, and so on. Promote appropriate use of medical services and active involvement in treatment decisions.

- Provide medical self-care education to reduce inappropriate medical utilization and improve patient-physician communication. Medical self-care programs can provide a 3:1 cost benefit within the first year of implementation, research shows.[54] Such programs commonly include home distribution of a self-care resource book or a Web-based resource; an orientation workshop or video; and regular, ongoing communications.

- Form a work group of employees who are key opinion leaders in your organization, whose task is to create a common mission and accomplish goals surrounding the health of individual workers. Include representatives from manufacturing, union, middle management, and so forth. The company's role will be to commit to investing in the proposed solutions. Through participation in this process, employees gain a stake in improved health and the ability to influence outcomes.

- Each year, give employees a confidential, voluntary scorecard, based on the results of their health risk appraisals, showing how their health has improved, remained the same, or deteriorated. As with a 401K plan, people like getting periodic statements on their accounts so they can see the results of their personal contributions.

- Celebrate someone who has complied with a disease management program, for example, by giving them a "healthy employee of the month" parking place or free lunch in the cafeteria for a week, or featuring their inspiring story in the employee newsletter (first get their permission and ask them to sign a confidentiality waiver). Offer other incentives to help drive participation and adherence. See Rule 6.

- Offer a disease management program for high-cost chronic illnesses. In its simplest form, you can hand out health information tailored to individual health needs or conditions, or provide targeted "information prescriptions" listing reputable Internet sites.

- Design a healthful corporate environment. Implement a smoke-free policy with the buy-in of your employees and management. Keep onsite vending machines stocked with low-fat snacks and bottled water. Price healthful cafeteria selections lower than high-fat, high-calorie foods.

Then, there are all the essentials of a corporate wellness program. You can implement anything from a full-scale, comprehensive program to a symbolic one that does little more than offer a newsletter, a membership subsidy at a local health club, or an educational Web site. At the very least, consider offering a core program that is communications based, has a visible brand identity, and reinforces a culture of health. Give it a name—Pitney Bowes called its program "Health Care University"; Union Pacific Corporation has its "HealthTrack"; Aetna has "Healthy Lifestyles"; Highsmith has "T.A.G."

Even as the program serves your high-risk employees, be sure you don't ignore the majority of your workforce who are healthy, low-risk employees. Think of your low-risk employees as what Dee W. Edington, Ph.D., of The University of Michigan's Health Management Research Center (HMRC) calls your company's *market share*.[55] By increasing your percentage of healthy employees, the value of your human assets appreciates, and the organization is able to leverage those assets for greater competitive advantage. What's more, it will cost you less to keep people well than to manage existing health conditions. The HMRC estimates that an organization saves $350 annually when a low-risk employee remains low risk, compared to a savings of $153 when a high-risk employee's health risks are reduced.[55]

Health risk appraisals (HRAs) and health screenings are the foundation of many health promotion programs because they are key to personal empowerment. Both of these strategies give immediate feedback about personal health, with strong justification for making health and lifestyle improvements. They will drive people to all your other offerings and are fairly inexpensive to implement.

Free and low-cost HRAs can be found online. Your health plan may offer one on its Web site; ask about any other wellness-related services the plan can offer your employees, such as a health promotion newsletter sent to employees' homes.

You also can work with a local hospital to offer periodic preventive screenings at your worksite, such as blood pressure readings and glucose and cholesterol tests. Or, get together with the human resources department at other companies to organize community-based activities. If you offered physicians $100 to participate in a health fair, chances are they would jump at the chance to see 200 prospective new patients in a two- to three-hour period.

Many employers are designing financial incentives into their health benefits plans to reward participation in HRAs and/or health screenings. Some offer a $150 rebate on an employee's premium contribution, for example, or an extra $50 for the person's flexible spending account toward purchasing prescription medications. Depending on your population, more symbolic incentives, such as T-shirts or mugs with your program logo, can be just as effective at driving behaviors.

To create a true culture of health, you will have to reinforce the message about the value of health every day—and it helps when employees see the CEO walking briskly through the hallways to get in his 10,000 steps a day.

All of these efforts can help to reinforce personal accountability throughout your organization. Importantly, they help to shift the attitude that health benefits are provided as an entitlement, to understanding that they are valuable tools requiring personal accountability and responsibility in their use.

Avoid barriers to effective treatment

GEORGE LEANED IN *toward Rebecca at the cafeteria table. "So what you're saying is, if we set up all the right conditions in the workplace, people will start assuming more personal responsibility—not only for their lifestyle habits, but also for how they use their health benefits."*

"That's right," Rebecca answered.

"That makes a lot of sense," he said. "So, is this the time when we can finally start talking about the nitty-gritty of health benefits design—you know, designing benefits to drive behaviors?"

"Great timing," she replied. "Would you like to begin?"

Who, me? George wondered. But then why not? He was the one who had first introduced Rebecca to the intricacies of benefits design. This was one area he knew something about.

"Well," he replied, "I suppose we can start with the basics and build from there. Where are we—rule number five? How about this: 'Make employees feel it in the pocketbook.' In order to help control costs and encourage personal responsibility, we need to increase copayments and other out-of-pocket costs, so people think twice before making inappropriate health care purchases."

That was too obvious, he thought. Rebecca didn't seem impressed.

"Well yes, that can be true to a certain extent."

"Can be true?"

"Actually," Rebecca said, "to help control our total costs, we have lowered some of the out-of-pocket costs to employees, particularly for prescription drugs and routine medical care. Sometimes we come close to giving medications away to the people who would most benefit from them."

"But—" George sputtered. "But … isn't that archaic? Lowering the out-of-pocket is counter to all the latest thinking in health cost containment and benefits design. Not to mention common sense. Lower the out-of-pockets, utilization increases. Increase utilization and costs increase. Didn't you attend the same conference I did last month?" He felt a lump forming in his throat.

"I know for sure you missed the Total Value *presentation," she said with a friendly laugh.*

George opened his mouth but nothing came out.

"One major employer saw its diabetes-related pharmaceutical costs alone drop by 7 percent after it lowered coinsurance for those pharmaceuticals," Rebecca continued. "Not to mention the savings it saw in reduced emergency room visits, disability days, and in lower overall health care costs. We're hoping for similar results ourselves. It may go against decades of thinking," she added, "but where has all that thinking gotten us? U.S. health care costs are still soaring. Pharmaceutical costs are still soaring."

"You do have to keep controlling the costs through benefits design," she stressed. "But the more you get to know about total value, the more it makes complete common sense to increase access to effective medical treatments and to avoid creating barriers. Let me explain."

When the World Trade Center was hit on September 11, 2001, Pitney Bowes was hit hard. We had roughly 100 people in the financial center at the time and another 700 employees in the surrounding vicinity. We were particularly concerned about the potential for depression among our employees. And then, just weeks later we got hit by anthrax—those mail services employees were Pitney Bowes workers.

All the systems we had in place, and our flexible mindset, allowed our response to these tragedies. The chairman said very simply, "Employees are our first responsibility." We did some pretty basic things right after 9-11: We took the call center that handles benefits and flipped it over to an employee support center. We quickly found ourselves in the grocery delivery business. We opened support services in New York and brought in employee assistance professionals. When anthrax came, the company used similar techniques. The amazing thing is that through both of these earth-shaking crises, we never saw any psychiatric difficulties among affected employees. We never saw an employee who refused to walk into a worksite. At the very least, our people trusted management that their health was not going to be affected adversely.

We received an award from the American Psychological Association for the way we supported employees right after 9-11. But it wasn't just about acting like the "good Samaritan"; it was about identifying the most urgent needs of our people, and *reducing any barriers* to what they needed.

The concept of lowering the barriers to effective treatment initially may be hard for most CEOs, CFOs, and benefits managers to accept. It can take some out-of-the-box thinking. But when done right, it actually can bring a very significant short-term payoff—plus it's perfectly aligned with the total value mission.

Everything should be about effective, lower-cost treatment that gets your people back to work and engaged the fastest. Whether an employee has been confronted by a catastrophic event or by a low-back injury from improper lifting, it's all about finding resources quickly, resolving care issues quickly, and getting people back into the field and engaged in their work.

Common Barriers

As Rule 4 revealed, even the highest-quality care loses its effectiveness when the employee doesn't adhere to it. Yet, most employers continue to design cost or access barriers into their benefits plans. They put up barriers not only to basic, effective treatments for heart disease, diabetes, asthma, and the like, but also to recommended health screenings, physicals, and other forms of primary prevention.

For example, an employer may:

- increase coinsurance to levels unaffordable to lower-paid workers.

- limit easy access to physicians, evidence-based practices, or other effective treatments by setting stringent pre-authorization requirements or high copays.

- fail to educate employees about how to communicate with their physicians, or how to manage chronic illness or common self-care issues.

- limit employees to a network of providers whose offices are too distant or are closed after normal work hours, or who don't speak the native language of ethnic employees.

- limit wellness programs to after hours.

Barriers such as these may cause people to avoid seeing a doctor until they've developed a costly, debilitating condition and no longer have a choice. This not only can increase health care costs exponentially, but also can lower productivity and increase absenteeism, workers' compensation, and disability costs.

As such, barriers that were implemented to reduce costs may, in fact, be increasing costs over both the short- and long-term.

Pharmaceutical Benefits Design

Removing barriers, in turn, can have a net effect of reducing costs. Pharmaceutical benefits are a classic example. Consider these research findings:

- While improved adherence to prescription drugs initially will increase medication expenditures, when it comes to high-cost chronic conditions, those added costs are likely to be more than offset by reductions in medical care costs, based on a recent study of more than 137,000 patients younger than 65.

The researchers found significantly lower hospitalization rates among patients with diabetes, hypertension, hypercholesterolemia, and congestive heart failure who had high medication adherence; and a net reduction in overall health care costs among high-adhering patients with diabetes, hypercholesterolemia, and hypertension.[56]

- Productivity may improve as well. In one study, the value of an unimpaired ability to work due to newer medications was measured across 47 major chronic health conditions. Over a 15-year study period, it was concluded that new medications demonstrated that savings from a significant increase (2.5 times) in employees' ability to work was greater than the expenditures for those medications.[57]

- Pitney Bowes itself has seen highly encouraging results from benefits designs that increase access to certain pharmaceuticals. Rather than charging more for all brand-name drugs in our three-tiered drug plan, we started offering every asthma, diabetes, and hypertension drug at Tier 1—meaning all those medications for chronic illnesses were provided at the same 10 percent coinsurance level offered for the less-expensive generic drugs, compared to the previous Tier 2 or 3 cost share of 30 percent to 50 percent. After two to three years, preliminary results are promising. For example, among plan participants with diabetes[58]:

–Medication adherence rates have increased significantly.

–Average total pharmacy costs have decreased by 7 percent.

–Emergency room visits have decreased by 26 percent.

–Hospital admission rates have increased slightly, but remain below our demographically-adjusted benchmark.

–Overall direct health care costs per plan participant for diabetes have decreased by 6 percent.

–Short-term disability days among employees in the diabetes program have been reduced by approximately 50 percent.[59]

In addition, at Pitney Bowes, we have experienced a markedly slowed increase in overall health costs per plan-participant—less than one-third the rate of inflation experienced by our competitors. We attribute much of the recent moderation of overall corporate health costs to our strategic redesign of drug benefits for diabetes, asthma, and hypertension, as well as to lower copayments for physician office visits, the availability of low-cost or free preventive screenings, and other, ongoing enhancements we've made to our disease management and wellness programs.

Meanwhile, we've seen no negative reaction among employees to lowering coinsurance for those who need it most. Intuitively, from every perspective the strategy makes good sense.

How Cost Affects Adherence

Multitier drug coverage is commonly used to drive patients toward lower-cost generic drugs by charging them a higher copay for brand-name medications. But this strategy can backfire when higher copays reduce the likelihood that a chronically ill patient will get a prescription filled or refilled, or take a medication as advised.[60-62]

As echoed in the World Health Organization's report entitled "Adherence to Long-term Therapies: Evidence for Action," "Medicines will not be effective if patients do not follow prescribed treatment, yet in developed countries only 50 percent of patients who suffer from chronic diseases adhere to treatment recommendations."[50] Partly, because of effective drugs recently introduced to the market, medications now play a major role in keeping symptoms of acute and chronic illness under control and preventing serious complications that can be very costly both to personal health and the corporate bottom line. In fact, pharmaceuticals are often the cheapest way to control chronic illnesses.

A study by the RAND Corporation found that the use of medications for diabetes, hypertension, and other chronic conditions were reduced when copayments were doubled. Patients with diabetes reduced their use of antidiabetes medications by 23 percent.[60] Our own internal research showed that the higher the tier (and thus the higher the out-of-pocket cost), the lower the rates of adherence, indicating that for our own employees, adherence was clearly a function of price.

How does price have this effect? Imagine you're an employee making $10 per hour, and your physician puts you on a drug that costs you $35 out-of-pocket compared to $10 for the generic. That $35 comprises more than three hours of work before taxes—and filling your prescription may mean the difference between filling up your gas tank to go to work or not. So you may cross your fingers and decide you'll make do without it. Or, if you do purchase the drug, you may try to stretch it out so you don't have to buy it again right away. For example, instead of following your doctor's instructions to take it every day, you may take it every two days, or cut your daily dosage in half.

If the drug is for high blood pressure, by skimping on it, you are putting yourself at higher risk of a serious cardiovascular event. If the drug is for asthma, you may have more trouble breathing. If it's for diabetes, you may experience more highs and lows from uncontrolled blood sugar, and get sick or pass out. In each case, you put your health at risk, and diminish your ability to engage productively in day-to-day activities at work and home.

The Pitney Bowes Experience

The potential payback of improved access to pharmaceuticals is within one year. We estimate that Pitney Bowes spends more than a million dollars per year to improve adherence to asthma, diabetes, and hypertension medications, and doing so saves at least that much in return.[61] This strategy also sends a very strong message to employees about how our organization values health. Not only are we telling people they need to be responsible for their own health and lifestyles, but we also are showing we are willing to invest in their health where it matters.

What we've seen in our company, which makes sense now a few years down the road, is that when people begin to adhere to their medication treatments they begin to feel better, and when they feel better there is less use of the emergency room by patients with diabetes, and fewer inpatient visits for asthma complications. Just as important, we've seen an overall reduction in pharmaceutical expenses, because many of these people have also been taking medications for co-morbid conditions—for example, unmanaged diabetes is often accompanied by hypertension or heart disease.[36]

However, we would never adjust copays upward or downward without first knowing our population and its needs. Not every medication should be low cost; and the potential return on investment is likely to vary considerably depending on the characteristics of a given population.

Pitney Bowes based its benefits redesign on predictive modeling. Our findings revealed that when an employee was diagnosed with diabetes, the person's health care and disability costs could quickly reach $10,000 a year. Yet surprisingly, the factor contributing most to those costs was not the presence of a chronic condition; it was the fact that people were not having their prescription medications filled. We found this true not only for diabetes, but also for asthma, hypertension, depression, and heart disease. In addition, we learned that as the out-of-pocket cost for medications increased, adherence decreased. Based on these findings we took a leap of faith and lowered the copay for all the drugs for those conditions. Often, patients ended up paying 80 percent less than before (e.g., 10 percent coinsurance rather than 50 percent). We had doubts that lowering out-of-pocket costs would actually drive behavior, since demand for health benefits typically is inelastic. But on receiving our first year's data in 2002, we saw our gamble had paid off in increased adherence.

Our pharmaceutical benefits design is built on a traditional three-tier formulary, and overall it achieves a 75 percent/25 percent cost sharing with employees. However, it has only limited prior authorization (required for just six drugs because of safety concerns), and it requires no mandatory generics, step therapy, or therapeutic substitution. Despite lack of controls, all our metrics are the same as in programs that have the controls in place. The cost incentive is very apparent to employees.

What Others Are Doing

A. Mark Fendrick, M.D., of the University of Michigan, Ann Arbor, arrived at this idea of enhanced access to pharmaceuticals independently of Pitney Bowes. Fendrick's premise is that one should assess the likely benefit a patient would receive from a given drug; compare that benefit to the potential total cost of treatment; and based on that analysis, establish lower copayments for patients who have clinical attributes similar to people for whom the drug has proven beneficial. Patients who are less likely to benefit could be charged higher but still moderate copayments.[62]

A growing number of large and small employers and municipalities are increasing access to pharmaceuticals for the same reason Pitney Bowes did—we believe it's a movement. Studies will be coming out soon to show the impact of their benefits redesign strategies. Smaller employers have a lot to gain from this option as well, based on the impressive results by the City of Asheville, North Carolina, from its Asheville Project.[63] The city discovered a high prevalence of diabetes among its employees, so in 1997 it launched a unique disease management program in collaboration with local pharmacists. In 1999, Mission-St. Joseph Health System joined the project. Participating employees agree to meet monthly with specially trained pharmacists who give them basic physical exams and help to ensure they adhere to medications and maintain their health. If a health problem is detected, the pharmacists promptly refer patients to their physicians. The pharmacists are reimbursed for their services.

Notably, participating patients make no copayments at all for the pharmacist visits, drugs for their disease, or other supplies. However, they are removed from the program and must begin making copayments again if they fail to adhere to program guidelines.

The results of the Asheville Project are significant: Total mean direct medical costs of participants with diabetes have decreased every year compared to the baseline. Participants' sick days have dropped by more than 50 percent and a higher percentage of participants have improved their clinical measures.[63]

Other Strategies for Lowering Barriers

As an employer's disease management interventions become well established, the next generation of value-based health care is to do everything possible in plan design to move chronically ill people to compliance with treatment. You can give them increased access to effective care without setting up a separate health plan for them. For example, you can require them to pay up front for medications, and then reimburse them later or deposit the money in a savings account for them. Those who follow the prescribed treatment patterns in their entirety should receive additional rewards.

Beyond pharmaceutical benefits design, here are some other ways to reduce barriers to effective medical care:

- **Offer preventive services and other routine care either for free or for a minimal copay, and have deductibles kick in after routine medical care.** Pitney Bowes was one of the first companies to do this with preventive care in all its health care plans. Today, about 10 percent of our total spending for direct medical services goes toward prevention—this is nearly unheard of among other employers.

  The number of our physician visits is high—and in a way, we look at that as a good thing. At some point in the history of benefits design, employers all got entranced by the idea that if you put in an up-front deductible for preventive care, you're going to save money. You may think it's wonderful when your people don't have health claims. But from our experience, low access to the health care system is one of our highest risks. Our own research showed that the employees most likely to become high-cost claimants in the year to come were those who spent more than $780 on health care and those who spent nothing (i.e., weren't having routine checkups). A middle-aged employee, for example, who doesn't access the health care system is at pretty high risk of becoming a high-cost claimant.

- **Improve access to EAP services.** Pitney Bowes discovered that its high out-of-pockets for employee assistance program services were contributing to absenteeism and direct health care costs. So, we did something that should be the norm; we increased the number of free EAP sessions offered to employees. When stress levels are high, sometimes people just need to talk to someone else about their personal concerns. We've also seen a positive impact from this change on the physical health side.

- **Overcome language and time barriers.** If your company has a high concentration of Asians, Hispanics, or other ethnic groups, shop around for a network of physicians and nurse practitioners who can speak their languages. In addition, educate these employees about how to access the health care system. Ask your health plan what services they offer. For example, Oxford Health Plan printed all its materials in Chinese and Spanish. If you're seeing high utilization of emergency room services, one solution may be to include in your network more providers with extended after-work hours.

- **Bring preventive services on site.** For many employees, geographical distance can be a major barrier to accessing routine health care. Think about asking your local public health department what it can offer your employees—whether it's onsite health screenings or a flu shot campaign.

- **Make wellness programs accessible.** Scheduling wellness programs after hours creates problems for working parents. Try scheduling them during the day, and use other programming options such as Web-based instruction.

Value-Based Decision Making

Whatever steps you take to reduce barriers to effective medical treatment, we suggest you adhere to this fundamental strategy: Instead of a big-bomb approach, aim for surgical strikes that will produce high impact, and therefore high value, to your organization and its employees. This means:

- Identify the major drivers of medical, disability, and workers' compensation costs in your organization—whether they are cancer, maternity, asthma, diabetes, back pain, or heart disease.

- Get to know employees' characteristics, their needs, their perceptions, and the barriers they face. Benefits managers aren't aware of many of these barriers simply because they don't ask.

- Work with your health plan to develop creative programs that will produce tangible results and will produce them quickly.

For example, increasing access to the most effective diabetes treatments may have the immediate, visible effect of reducing costly hospital visits. Yet, improved adherence to hypertension medication or cholesterol-lowering drugs is unlikely to show any tangible return on investment because of the lack of outward symptoms for these conditions. In the latter case, regardless of its value, your investment in improved access will be seen as "just another benefits project" implemented by someone unwilling to make the tough business decisions.

When upper management starts seeing you do targeted interventions with quick, clear results, you'll gain instant credibility. As a result, your future efforts will receive more support, and you'll be positioned to win the war, not just the battle. You'll be able to operate in a very open environment, and you'll be gaining new skills that will make you more employable.

Have you ever done a focus group with employees to see how they access care in their local community? If you would do that, chances are you will get some revealing feedback. You can ask your health plan to give you data about utilization of services broken down by geography, ethnicity, family status, and income. When you see the results, you can then create a series of working hypotheses or assumptions. Then, talk to people.

You don't need a formal focus group. Just walk the floor and ask: When was the last time you went to the doctor for a physical? Were office hours convenient? Did they speak your language? Was it hard to get an appointment? At certain physicians' offices, you have to book an appointment six months in advance, which can lead people to the emergency room.

Common Sense

We tell people over and over that removing barriers to effective treatment is not a simple matter of changing the formulary. For Pitney Bowes, doing that was only a piece of the puzzle, albeit the piece that garnered us the most publicity. A total approach is necessary, and it begins with understanding your people.

Most importantly, ensure that your benefits design does not overly limit access to effective, appropriate treatment. Look holistically at reducing barriers, and apply a strong dose of common sense. If it costs 10 cents per person to reduce the barrier and it will have a clear impact on improving health and productivity—saving money and saving lives—would you spend it? If the answer is yes, then you're on your journey to value-based decision making. In the area of pharmaceuticals, you may end up spending more than 10 cents, but the investment will still be a low percentage of the total cost for managing that condition than for office visits, hospitalizations, and other services.

Our CEO, Mike Critelli, has an open mind, and each time we present a new creative idea to him, he tends to think it through. Often, he'll beat us to the punch.

The caveat is, monitor your actions and your results. Don't create an open exposure around costs. At the same time, unless you explore, you're not going to find.

Carrots are valued over sticks

"IF I COULD BE BACK in the business of offering benefits again," George mused, "offering something of real value to employees, something that makes their whole lives better at work and home ... and yet still be delivering real value to the bottom line .... This is great stuff, Rebecca," he announced.

Then he noticed the time: "Darn. I want to talk to you more about this, but if I don't get back soon my boss will think I'm out job hunting."

He was only half joking. But then it flashed in his mind that perhaps he had just landed himself a new job—at Nuts & Bolts. If he could really internalize what he'd learned over the past weeks, test it out in earnest, and start accumulating tangible results, this could be a brand new beginning. Suddenly he couldn't wait to get back and plan out his week.

"Tell you what," Rebecca said. "If you stay just a few minutes longer I'll treat you to dessert. We can take it upstairs to HR. Then you'll get the rest of the 25-cent tour, and I'll drive you back to your office."

He really did have to go. But dessert—well ... "That carrot cake did look pretty appetizing," he agreed with a smile.

Up in Rebecca's office, George sat back, took a sip of coffee, and gazed past the curtains. A walking trail wound around the rear of the building, occasional signs marking it. Several folks were down there walkng. He took a bite of carrot cake and tried to spot Jerry on the trail.

"Many of those people wouldn't be out there right now if their health were the only reason," Rebecca said. "Most people normally are far too busy for physical activity."

Like I am, George thought to himself. "That is rather remarkable. How did you get them out there?"

"The same way I got you up here," she said with a laugh. "We offer a carrot. Not carrot cake, but a financial incentive. If they complete our healthy lifestyle challenge, they get $150 off of their health premiums for the year."

"I'd walk around the building for that," George remarked. He took another bite of cake.

"For some populations a T-shirt or a gift certificate can be just as effective," she added. "The incentive is the magical ingredient, the catalyst that sets all the wheels in motion. Some employers offer disincentives," Rebecca added, "like higher premiums for unhealthy behaviors. But employees value carrots over sticks."

Once you've installed the walking trail around the building, once you've put healthy foods in the cafeteria and in the vending machines, once you've got all the right benefits in place and you've reduced the barriers to effective treatment, then you need to add the carrot.

It's human nature. Most people require an added incentive to move out of their comfort zone and change ingrained behaviors. Even many health care providers need an incentive to deliver higher-quality, lower-cost care.

You can offer employees a T-shirt for achieving a specified number of health goals, or a premium rebate for successfully completing a program for smoking cessation or asthma management. You can hold a prize drawing for participants in an onsite health screening, or publicize someone's accomplishment in the employee newsletter. You can offer time off from work, a gift certificate to an online store, or, as discussed previously, a lower copayment for selective medications.

Cash rewards linked to benefits have particularly broad appeal and high relevance. A. Mark Fendrick, M.D., of the University of Michigan has said, "The beauty of the [benefits-based copayment] system is its ability to reflect the values of a particular health plan or employer."[62] Benefits-linked incentives deliver a strong message about health as a core value, since they align both behavior and reward to health. Many employers offer such an incentive to employees who participate in an annual or biannual health risk appraisal, for example, by depositing $100 to $150 in a flexible spending account.

Carrots or Sticks

Some employers have taken the approach of penalizing workers for poor health practices such as smoking. However, carrots are valued over sticks, and sticks are not particularly effective over time. Instead of reinforcing positive behaviors (and the value of good health), disincentives place the focus on negative behaviors and on the outliers with entrenched habits.

In every population, around 10 percent of people will be outside the norm. No matter what carrot you offer, they will maintain a strong resistance to change. You'll have better results by keeping your focus planted on the people who are more open to adopting or maintaining healthy behaviors. Your low-risk population is your market share, and they also must be supported in staying low risk. The old adage serves well here: An ounce of prevention is worth a pound of cure. While taking steps to improve efficiency and value in your health management strategies, you may as well get it right from the start.

Keep in mind that cost barriers to effective medical treatment can be perceived intuitively as a form of punishment for choosing higher-cost options, such as brand-name medications.

There is a valid argument that long-term behavior change can be driven only from within, not externally. Clearly, however, incentives work at least in the short term, and they are ideal for jumpstarting new behaviors. They work best when they deliver a consistent message and are designed properly as part of your broader program strategy. They must be aligned with the distinctive needs and interests of your target audience, with corporate values of health, and with the goal of achieving total return on your investment in health.

Examples of Incentives

The Asheville Project, discussed on page 51, is a prime example of how benefits-linked incentives can succeed in getting chronically ill patients to monitor and manage their conditions more effectively. Participating city employees learn quickly that if they want to pay nothing out of pocket for services, medications, and supplies, they have to do something in return for the employer, such as meeting monthly with a specially trained pharmacist and receiving basic health screenings. This project also shows how an employer-designed program can encourage pharmacists to provide low-cost, high-quality disease management services. During the 5-year study period, the diabetes program has saved the city between $1,200 and $1,872 per patient per year.[63]

Health Care University (HCU), Pitney Bowes' own, onsite health improvement program, is another example of how incentives can be positioned within a broader strategy. This program bridges demand management, disability management, and disease management and prevention as it motivates healthy behaviors among employees. The program changes yearly, but its basic thrust remains the same: Participants earn credits by participating in selected activities, and if they earn enough credits (e.g., 6) during the allotted time, they are awarded a cash value toward future benefits purchases. Normally, the incentive works out to a 10 percent discount in the following year's health benefits. In any given year, one in four employees will earn the incentive. Over a 3-year period, the program saved Pitney Bowes $3 in health care costs for every $1 invested.

All activity in the HCU program is self-reported, which is in line with treating people like adults. Eligible behaviors include basic things like wearing safety belts, being a nonsmoker (or participating in a smoking cessation program), participating in nutrition counseling, health screening, or a health risk appraisal. Aggregate data from the health risk assessment are used for targeting future programs; but the primary purpose of this instrument is to inform, motivate, and empower the individual.

As you'll discover in Rule 7, ideally the incentives for purchaser, patient, and provider will be aligned. The Bridges to Excellence program (page 29) shows how employers can create this alignment. Not only does Bridges to Excellence reward physicians with recognition and cash incentives for delivering high quality and high efficiency at a lower cost, but in some cases, patients also receive an incentive for choosing to receive care from a recognized physician. Through the program's Diabetes Care Link, rewards also encourage employees and family members to be more active in managing their conditions; when they use certain available tools, they receive cash, discounted copayments or other incentives.[47]

Setting the Wheels in Motion

Try experimenting with different incentives. Just keep in mind that in order to get top value from incentives, you need to:

- **Be results oriented.** As with any health management initiative in which you consider investing, project the potential impact that incentives have on the cost of benefits, disability days, the functional health of employees, and any other strategic measures.

- **Align incentives with the intended behaviors.** To do so requires having a clear understanding of the behaviors you want to drive. If your goal is improved adherence to effective treatment for depression, for example, consider that experts often recommend that optimal treatment is a combination of both medication and psychotherapy. Therefore, if the only incentive you offer is a lower copayment for medication, your employees may be encouraged to over-medicate themselves. To target the incentive more carefully, you might tie it to a caregiver visit. For example: When someone visits an EAP counselor or a psychologist, the provider could hand him or her a coupon toward a lower out-of-pocket cost for medication.

- **Drive adherence.** Incentives often are used to drive participation; but more specifically they should drive adherence, whether adherence to a regular walking program or to a prescribed asthma medication.

Include carrots for dependents and spouses. When an employee is overweight or sedentary, or has diabetes or asthma, multiple family members typically share the same condition or risk factors. In addition, lifestyle change is especially difficult when you live with people who maintain their unhealthy habits. To involve family members, send educational information to the home and offer home-based programs, with appropriate incentives to drive the behaviors of all.

- **Avoid a perception of entitlement.** Make it clear that incentives, like all your programs, are under constant review and are likely to be modified from time to time.

Ultimately, understand that incentives are essential for helping your total value initiatives run like clockwork. They are what sets all the other wheels in motion. Incentives are key to participation, adherence, and completion. They are all about messaging, and about aligning design with desired behaviors.

Total value demands total teamwork

"SO ARE YOU READY to put all this into your own words now?" Rebecca asked George.

"Ready as I can be," he answered. "But you'll be delivering the opening spiel, right?"

Two months after his tour of Profitable Bank, George was sitting with Rebecca, along with Scott, the HR director of Superb Engineering, in the front offices of XYZ Health Plan. George and Scott had each visited here once before, but not with such a lofty purpose. Rebecca herself was here to renew a former relationship with the health plan and bring them up to speed.

"By the way," George mentioned quietly to Rebecca, "I met yesterday afternoon with the CEO."

He paused for dramatic effect.

"He gets it!" he announced. "He's going to back me in designing programs and benefits to manage our asthma and diabetes costs. Today's meeting is timely, wouldn't you say? What really strikes me," George added, "is how impressed he was with my grasp of total costs, and of how we can use strategic benefits design to contribute to the bottom line. He pressed me to move forward immediately, and he's increasing my budget!"

They were interrupted by a woman and a tall gentleman entering the room. After introductions, Rebecca, George, and Scott were ushered into a conference room, where Rebecca began the meeting.

"Thank you for this opportunity to meet with you here today," she said. "As I mentioned over the phone, all of us have a shared purpose: Profitable Bank, Nuts & Bolts, Superb Engineering, all *the many people who work for us, and of course, XYZ Health Plan. We all have a goal of better health, and of lower health care costs. Does everyone agree?"*

With all in accord, she took her place by an easel and launched immediately into a distillation of total value. She discussed the impact of direct and indirect health care costs, the value of human assets, quality of care, shared accountability, barriers to effective treatment, incentives, and more. She laid it all out like a pro.

"So you see," she explained to the health plan representatives, "it is our firm intention to give our combined business to the health plans that deliver not just the lowest cost, but also the highest value for our health care dollar. We realize this is asking something new and unfamiliar of XYZ, but together we can make it happen. The critical thing is, total value demands total teamwork. We can't achieve total value and total return in isolation. We need you to be our partner in this."

As George glanced at the account reps, he saw in each of their faces a new expression of genuine respect. He felt great. George, Rebecca, and Scott together represented more than 3,000 local employees, and the power of those numbers was palpable. They were about to ask XYZ Health Plan some tough business questions, and XYZ was going to listen and respond. Benefits design was fun, George thought to himself. Something quite remarkable was about to happen here....

Total value demands total teamwork. If we employers are going to shift from a culture of managing disease to one of managing health, there needs to be a consensus of shared accountability among employer, employee, and health plan/provider. It's like a three-legged stool: If one of the legs doesn't hold up its end of the bargain, the entire effort collapses.

As it is, because the health care market is not subject to normal dynamics of supply and demand, all three stakeholders have taken to functioning in their own private silos with little shared information among them and no clear common purpose. Employees can be brought up to speed as we discussed in Rule 4. Now, it's time to discuss how to enlist health plans in a strategy of total teamwork.

Creating a Dynamic Relationship

The first step toward creating symmetry is a simple one: Identify the lowest common denominator that links all players to a common purpose, and then communicate that common denominator to all. At Pitney Bowes, we begin with the premise that a healthy employee is key to a healthy organization. Then we take a step back and ask: Toward achieving the goal of a healthy employee, what is the responsibility of the employer? The responsibility of the individual? The responsibility of the health plan/provider? And where are the opportunities for their roles to overlap?

The Need for Transparency

Once opportunities have been identified, it is important that relevant data be collected, evaluated, and shared among key stakeholders in order to facilitate a value-based decision-making process. In other words, there needs to be *transparency* in not only sharing data, but also in aligning goals and incentives based on the data. In doing so, the decision-making process will most likely be shortened and more proactive. In addition, because of transparency, decisions will be based on shared accountability by which all parties share the risks and rewards of a selective initiative.

The Need for Shared Accountability

If employee (organizational) health is viewed as a key success factor for creating total value and total return in an organization, then this requires shared accountability among key stakeholders in achieving defined goals. This relationship can be depicted as a triad.

Generally speaking:

- The employer is responsible for targeting the needs of its people and designing appropriate services (benefits) that will drive the actions of both employees and the health plan/provider.

- The employee is responsible for the appropriate use of health care resources and for engaging in healthy behaviors.

- The health plan/provider is responsible for executing the plan design, managing data, and ensuring it delivers appropriate, high-quality services and care.

Goal	Employer responsibility	Employee responsibility	Plan/Provider responsibility
Increased access	Plan design	Plan selection	Plan execution
Personal accountability	Communication	Informed decision-making and self-management	Physician-patient communication
Quality of care	Incentives	Adherence	Quality
Knowing your population	Data mining	Health risk appraisal	Data management
Healthy behaviors	Environmental supports	Self-management	Access to appropriate care

Pitney Bowes and many other larger employers who are self-insured rely on external pharmacy benefits managers (PBM) to administer prescription benefits; as such, keep PBMs in mind when considering issues of health plan responsibility.

To get health plans and PBMs invested in achieving your goals, you must create a strong partnership with them. It helps when you have several thousand employees; but companies of fewer than 300 employees also can gain leverage by banding together with other like-minded employers, as George and Rebecca did. These formal or informal coalitions also may provide good opportunities for group purchasing, especially on the pharmacy benefits.

Don't hesitate to ask your managed care organization tough questions, such as: "What are you doing to work with me to manage our high-cost health conditions?" "What are you doing to ensure physicians in your network provide the best quality of care?" "What kinds of performance criteria have you established?" You are no longer just providing them with funding and signing on the dotted line; you are now asking the plan to work with you in reengineering its entire approach to benefits design.

In the end, everything comes back to your employees. Present to the health plan: This is what my employees need. How can you help me deliver it to them? Back and forth with the health plan, push and pull if you must. Reach a mutual understanding, then establish a service-level agreement so you both are held accountable for your actions. At the very least, open a dialog. Nearly any health plan is willing to come to your worksite and offer screenings or flu shots. You've got to start somewhere in developing a working partnership.

Many pharmaceutical plans also do screenings, and many have existing disease-management or educational programs. It can be to your advantage to utilize these services, as long as you enter the arrangement with clear principles so you don't end up promoting a specific drug or health plan to employees.

Be aware that the health plan can't meet every request you'll have, since some of your proposed financial incentives may not mesh with their business interests. The key is to establish that lowest common denominator, and build from there. Just ensure that any incentives you create are driving employees' behaviors toward your goal and communicating health as a core value of your organization.

Keep in mind, as well, that all health management decisions should be positioned from a perspective of total value, not on cost alone. Thus, you may have to invest in increased spending up front in order to realize a total return through reduced direct medical costs, lower absenteeism or disability, and sustained productivity on the job (e.g., less presenteeism).

Total Teamwork in Action

Pitney Bowes believes plan design is one of the key levers in the dynamic relationship among employer, employee, and health plan/provider. A design that gives the employee incentives to adhere to high-value care, and that also gives the provider incentives to offer high-value care, is the one that gets and keeps our business.

Our designs are set up to drive specific behaviors, particularly in terms of adherence to medications for chronic conditions. Because employees receive our communications and understand the financial incentives we've put in place, they now have changed their behaviors and have begun to increase their levels of adherence for asthma and diabetes. We soon will begin sharing our adherence data with our health plans so they can start scoring their providers on quality metrics and then link those scores to provider incentives. In other words, data needs to be transparent. In this way, data sharing serves as a wakeup call to patient and doctor alike: Is the patient taking his medications, and if not, why not? Our plan design and the sharing of pertinent information brings the physician, health plan, employee, and employer into full alignment toward a common purpose.

Perhaps you can see now why we've placed this rule—*total value demands total teamwork*—last among the seven. Basically, Rule 7 connects the dots among the other six rules. It reveals total value, total return with all gears engaged and the motor humming. The dynamic relationship among stakeholders drives appropriate treatment and healthy behavior change; and this, in turn, moves you along in the journey to smaller medical cost increases. As your organization's costs moderate, more funds will be freed up to invest in people through training and technology, through other new programs, and through new hires. This is how total teamwork, and total value, help your organization to stay competitive and flourish within the global marketplace.

SOMETIME IN THE FUTURE, *George is back in the coffee shop sipping on a latte, reflecting on all the costs he's saved his company through value-based benefits design. In walks Joe, the benefits manager for a local supermarket chain.*

"George? Haven't seen you since that conference two years ago. What have you been up to?"

"A lot," George replies. "Hey Joe, your company contracts with XYZ Health Plan, right? I was thinking of calling you, and maybe getting together with you to talk about some new ideas I have. Have you got a few minutes?"

And Joe sits down with George to learn about total value, total return.

Welcome to the final pages of *Total Value • Total Return*™. Now you have the ability and the tools to start applying this vision to your own benefits design.

Half the battle is focusing on measuring value rather than cost alone. The question is, do you want to be a part of the journey, or do you want to wait? The longer you wait, the larger the potential cost increases will be to your organization.

As you've learned by reading this far, there is real hope for the future. How you set your benefits design, how you interact with your health plans, how you interact with employees and other employers, can drive a culture focused on health and not on health costs, and can make your organization more competitive.

These are some of the key points you need to keep in mind:

- Human assets are the engine that drives the competitive advantage of your organization. Health, both physical and mental, is a critical success factor in gainful employment for the individual as well as in the health of your organization.

- Health benefits should be positioned and designed to create a culture of health within the organization. This requires a shift from illness management to health management.

- The cornerstone of this position is the organization's support for individuals in managing their health, regardless of their stage on the health care continuum. While you are helping high-risk, high-cost employees to access the care they need and self-manage their conditions, you also must focus on keeping the well, well.

- Your current benefits design may be creating barriers to effective health management. Reducing those barriers can enhance the total value of human assets and, in turn, increase the total return of their output and your investment.

- You can't make change happen in isolation. A full partnership among employer, employee, and health plan/provider is necessary.

Change happens at a local level, and change begins with you. Once you move into this arena, other employers and health plans will follow. Within just a few years you may witness the whole market moving upward.

Where Are You on the Journey?

The following checklist, based on the seven rules, will challenge you to examine how health-related benefits are designed and positioned within your organization's human capital management strategy. Check all that apply.

How do we approach the business of benefits design?

❑ We view health as a core value in our organization.

❑ We see health benefits as a tool that provides value not only to employees, but also to customers and shareholders.

❏ Health benefits are positioned not only as a way to manage direct health costs, but also as a way to invest in the health and productivity of our people, and therefore the health of our entire organization.

How do we target our benefits design?

❏ When designing benefits, we take into account the health conditions that are the top drivers of direct health care costs in our organization.

❏ We take into account the leading health risks of our employees and their dependents, both company-wide and for each company location.

❏ We take into account the primary health-related interests of our workers, based on employee surveys.

❏ Toward an understanding of total health care costs, we factor in the top drivers of at least one of these indirect costs of poor health: short-term disability, workers' compensation, absenteeism, and/or presenteeism.

❏ We are aware of the barriers that limit employees' access to appropriate, effective medical treatment (e.g., unaffordable coinsurance levels, distance or language barriers, restrictive networks, etc.).

How do we empower employees in the appropriate use of their benefits and in adopting appropriate health behaviors?

❏ We emphasize to employees their shared ownership in personal and organizational health.

- ❏ Our workplace environment promotes a healthy culture (e.g., healthy cafeteria selections, smoke-free policy, fitness trail, other wellness programs, disease management programs).

- ❏ We educate employees about how to communicate with their physicians and how to manage chronic illness or common medical self-care issues.

- ❏ We design benefits to reduce, not create, barriers to effective treatments, especially preventive care or treatment for chronic illness.

- ❏ We offer health screenings and/or health risk appraisals to employees in order to increase their personal health awareness and motivate them to choose healthy behaviors.

- ❏ We offer incentives to employees for adopting healthy behaviors or accessing appropriate, effective treatment.

How do we engage our health plans in benefits design?

- ❏ In discussions with health plans, we emphasize employee health and quality of care, including use of evidence-based treatment. Thus, we are focusing not only on low-cost services, but also on high-value services.

- ❏ We interact with other local employers to develop and promote quality of care initiatives by health plans/providers.

1. Gilmer T, Kronick R. It's the premiums, stupid: projections of the uninsured through 2013. *Health Affairs—Web exclusive.* April 2005.

2. Anderson G, Horvath J. The growing burden of chronic disease in America. *Public Health Reports.* 4004;119:263–270.

3. Heffler S, Smith S, Keehan S, et al. U.S. health spending projections for 2004–2014. *Health Affairs—Web exclusive.* 23 February 2005.

4. National Coalition on Health Care. Health insurance cost. http://www.nchc.org/facts/cost.shtml. Last accessed 2/15/06.

5. Gabel J, Claxton G, Gil I, et al. Health benefits in 2005: premium increases slow down, coverage continues to erode. *Health Affairs.* 2005;24(5):1273–1280.

6. Fullerton HN. Labor force projections to 2008: steady growth and changing composition. *Monthly Labor Review.* November 1999.

7. Health and Human Services. The Surgeon General's call to action to prevent and decrease overweight and obesity. http://surgeongeneral.gov/topics/obesity/calltoaction/1_4html. Last accessed 2/15/06.

8. Thorpe KE, Curtis SF, Howard DH, et al. The rising prevalence of treated disease: effects on private health insurance. *Health Affairs–Web exclusive.* June 2005.

9. National Mental Health Association. www.nmha.org/infoctr/factsheets/41.cfm. Last accessed 2/15/06.

10. Pelletier B, Boles M, Lynch W. Change in health risks and work productivity over time. *J Occup Environ Med.* 2004;46(7):746–754.

11. Aetna Life and Casualty. C. Everett Koop National Health Awards. http://healthproject.stanford.edu/koop/aetna/description.html. Last accessed 2/19/06.

12. Burton WN, Conti DJ, Chen CY, Schultz AB, Edington DW. The impact of allergies and allergy treatment on worker productivity. *J Occup Environ Med.* 2001;43(1):64–71.

13. Burton WN, Conti DJ, Chen-CY, et al. The role of health risk factors and disease on worker productivity. *J Occup Environ Med.* 1999;41(10):863–877.

14. Burton WN, Pransky G, Conti DJ, et al. The association of medical conditions and presenteeism. *J Occup Environ Med.* 2004;46(6) suppl:S38–S45.

15. Burton WN, Morrison A, Wertheimer AI. Pharmaceuticals and worker productivity loss: a critical review of the literature. *J Occup Environ Med.* 2003;45(6):610–621.

References

16. Burton WN, Conti DJ, Chen CY, et al. The economic burden of lost productivity due to migraine headache: a specific worksite analysis. *J Occup Environ Med.* 2002;44(6):523–529.

17. Burton WN, Hutchinson S, Helgeson L, et al. An evaluation of a worksite prenatal education program: five-year experience. *Worksite Health.* 2000;7(10):30–33.

18. The Corporate Health Achievement Award. Presented by the American College of Occupational and Environmental Medicine. 2005; www.chaa.org. Last accessed 2/15/06.

19. Dow Employee Health Programs and Services. http://www.dow.com/commitments/responsibility/health.html. Last accessed 2/18/06.

20. Baase CM. Effect of chronic health conditions on work performance and absence, and total economic impact for employers. *Health and Productivity Management.* 2005;4(3):14–16.

21. Senate Special Committee on Aging. June 30, 2005 Hearing testimony. http://aging.senate.gov/public/_files/hr145bh.pdf. Last accessed2/24/06.

22. Adams S. Making Intel health and productivity a global success. *Health and Productivity Management.* 2005;4(2):9–11.

23. Pfeiffer GJ. Keeping on track. *Worksite Health.* 2001;8(2):4–7.

24. Loeppke R, Hymel PA, Lofland JH, et al. Health-related workplace productivity measurement: general and migraine-specific recommendations from the ACOEM expert panel. *J Occup Environ Med.* 2003;45(4):349–359.

25. Edington DW, Burton WN. *Health and productivity. A Practical Approach to Occupational and Environmental Medicine.* Lippincott, Williams and Wilkins. Third edition. 2003;140–152.

26. Goetzel RZ. Examining the value of integrating occupational health and safety and health promotion programs in the workplace. *National Institute of Occupational Safety and Health.* 2005:1-61. http://www.cdc.gov/niosh/steps/pdfs/BackgroundPaper GoetzelJan2005.pdf Last accessed 6/25/05.

27. Goetzel RZ, Hawkins K, Ozminkowski RJ, et al. The health and productivity cost burden of the "top 10" physical and mental health conditions affecting six large U.S. employers in 1999. *J Occup Environ Med.* 2001;45(1):5–14.

28. Cash B, Sullivan S, Barghout V. Total costs of IBS: Employer and managed care perspective. *Am J Manag Care.* 2005;11(1):S7–S16.

29. Dean BB, Aquilar D, Barghout V, et al. Impairment in work productivity and health-related quality of life in patients with IBS. *Am J Manag Care,* 2005;11(1):S17–S26.

30. Smith DG, Barghout V, Kahler KH. Tegaserod treatment for IBS: a model for indirect costs. *Am J Manag Care.* 2005;11(1):S43–S50.

31. American Academy of Allergy, Asthma, and Immunology (AAAAI). *The Allergy Report: Science Based Findings on the Diagnosis & Treatment of Allergic Disorders, 1996–2001.* Cited by: American Academy of Allergy Asthma, and Immunology, "Asthma Statistics." See http://www.aaaai.org/media/resources/media_kit/allergy_statistics.stm. Last accessed 1/9/06

32. Bunn WB, Pikelny DB, Paralkar S, et al. The burden of allergies—and the capacity of medications to reduce this burden—in a heavy manufacturing environment. *J Occup Environ Med.* 2003;45(9):941–955.

33. American Lung Association. Trends in asthma morbidity and mortality. American Lung Association Epidemiology & Statistics Unit, Research and Scientific Affairs. March 2003.

34. Kessler RC, Greenburg PE, Mickelson K, et al. The effects of chronic medical conditions on work loss and work cutback. *J Occup Environ Med.* 2001;43(3):218–225.

35. Kessler RC, Barber C, Birnbaum HG, et al. Depression in the workplace: effects on short-term disability. *Health Affairs.* 1999;18:163–171.

36. The American Diabetes Association. National diabetes fact sheet, 2005. http://www.diabetes.org/diabetes-statistics.jsp. Last accessed 2/22/06

37. American Diabetes Association. Economic costs of diabetes in the U.S. in 2002. *Diabetes Care.* 2003;26:917–932.

38. Lee PY, Matchar DB, Clements DA. Economic analysis of influenza vaccination and antiviral treatment for healthy working adults. *Ann Intern Med.* 2002;137:225–231.

39. Bridges CB, Harper SA, Fukuda K, et al. Prevention and control of influenza. Centers for Disease Control and Prevention. 2003;52(RR08):1–36. http://www.cdc.gov/mmwr/preview/mmwrhtml/rr5208a1.htm. Last accessed 2/15/06.

40. Kaniecki R. Headache assessment and management. *JAMA.* 2003;289(11):1430–1433.

References

41. Kessler RC, Ormel J, Demler O, at al. Comorbid mental disorders account for the role impairment of commonly occurring chronic physical disorders: results from the national comorbidity survey. *J Occup Environ Med.* 2003;45(12):1257–1266.

42. Reinhardt UE, Hussey PS, Anderson GF. U.S. health care spending in an international context. *Health Affairs.* 2004;23(3):10–24.

43. Hussey PS, Anderson GF, Osborn R., et al. How does quality of care compare in five countries? *Health Affairs.* 2004;23(3):89–99.

44. Schoen C, Osborn R, Huynh Trang P, et al. Taking the pulse of health care systems: experiences of patients with health problems in six countries. *Health Affairs—Web Exclusive.* 3 November 2005.

45. Institute of Medicine. *Unequal Treatment. Confronting Racial and Ethnic Disparities in Health Care.* ed. Smedley B.D., Stith A.Y., Nelson A.R. National Academy Press, Washington, DC. 2002.

46. Davis K. Toward a high performance health system: the Commonwealth Fund's new commission. *Health Affairs.* 2005;24(5):1357–1360.

47. Bridges to Excellence. http://www.bridgestoexcellence.org. Last accessed 2/19/06.

48. McGlynn EA, Asch SM, Adams J, Keesey J, et al. The quality of health care delivered to adults in the United States. *N Engl J Med.* 2003;348:2635–2645.

49. The Leapfrog Group. http://www.leapfroggroup.org/about_us/leapfrog-factsheet. Last accessed 2/24/06.

50. The World Health Organization. *Adherence to Long-term Therapies: Evidence for Action.* 2005. http://www.who.int/chronic_conditions/adherencereport/en/print.html. Last accessed 2/15/06.

51. Dunbar-Jacob J. University of Pittsburgh, in a March 12, 2005, address to the U.S. Congress sponsored by the Coalition for the Advancement of Health Through Behavioral and Social Science Research (CAHT-BSSR), along with the Decade of Behavior, the American Psychological Association, COSSA, the Federation of Behavioral, Psychological, and Cognitive Sciences, and the Society for Research in Child Development. http://www.cossa.org/caht-bssr/selfmanagement.htm. Last accessed 2/15/06

52. Pfeiffer GJ. *Taking Care of Today and Tomorrow. A Resource Guide for Health, Aging, and Long-Term Care.* The Center for Corporate Health Promotion. Reston, Virginia. 1989.

53. Office of Personnel Management. High deductible health plans (HDHP) with health savings accounts (HSA). 2005. http://www.opm.gov/hsa/chart.asp. Last accessed 2/20/06.

54. Vickery DM, Kalmer H, Lowry D, et al. Effect of a self-care education program on medical visits. *JAMA.*1984;250:2952–2956.

55. University of Michigan Health Management Research Center. *The Worksite Wellness Cost Benefit Analysis and Report 2004.* 2004;1–22.

56. Sokol JC, McGuigan KA, Verbrugge RR, et al. Impact of medication adherence on hospitalization risk and healthcare cost. *Medical Care.* 2005;43:521–530.

57. Lichtenberg FR. Availability of new drugs and Americans' ability to work. *J Occup Environ Med.* 2005;47:373–380.

58. Mahoney JJ. Reducing patient drug acquisition costs can lower diabetes health claims. *Am J Manag Care.* 2005;11:S170–S176.

59. Mahoney JJ. Role of employer and health plan in disease management. Presentation to National Business Coalition on Health. January 19, 2006.

60. Goldman DP, Joyce GF, Escarce JJ, et al. Pharmacy benefits and the use of drugs by the chronically ill. *JAMA.* 2004;291(19):2344–2349.

61. Fuhrmans V. A radical prescription. While most companies look to slash health costs by shifting more expenses to employees, Pitney Bowes took a different tack. The results were surprising. *The Wall Street Journal.* May 10, 2004; R3.

62. Sipkoff M. Not so much of a reach: let sick pay less for drugs. *Managed Care.* 2004; 10:22–28.

63. Cranor CW, Bunting BA, Christensen DB. The Ashville Project: long-term clinical and economic outcomes of a community pharmacy diabetes program. *JAPhA.* 2003; 43(2):173–184.

64. *Human Capital,Your Greatest Asset: Building Effective Strategies to Protect, Support and Enhance Workplace Health and Productivity.* GlaxoSmithKline. Philadelphia, Penna. 2005.

Adherence. The ongoing persistence of an individual to follow recommended treatment guidelines such as medication use and appropriate lifestyle practices.

Brand drugs. A class of drugs identified by name as the product of a single firm or manufacturer.

Barriers to care. Factors (e.g., cost, access, health literacy, behavioral) that prevent an individual from complying or adhering to recommended treatment guidelines.

Coinsurance. The amount (percentage) patients have to pay for reasonable medical expenses after a deductible has been paid.

Competitive advantage. Advantage over competitors gained by offering consumers greater value, either by means of lower prices or by providing greater benefits and service that justifies higher prices.

Consumer Driven Health Plan (CDHP). A high-deductible health plan, that includes an employer-funded account to be used for employee health care needs. Many plans offer health savings accounts or health reimbursement accounts.

Copayment. A flat fee paid by the patient to a provider or pharmacy for each visit or prescription.

Deductible. A patient pays the full cost of benefits until an annual maximum is reached after which further costs are either shared or fully covered by the plan.

Demand management. Influencing the demand for medical services through decision support (e.g., nurse line) to promote appropriate care-seeking behavior (e.g., outpatient visit vs. emergency room utilization).

Direct Health Care Costs. Dollars paid directly for medical services such as outpatient care, hospitalization, pharmacy, and workers' compensation.

Disease management. Promoting the appropriate and timely use of screening, evaluation, and treatment regimens in the medical management of specific health conditions such as diabetes and depression.

Employee Assistance Program (EAP). A confidential and voluntary support service designed to provide assistance to employees and their dependents who may be facing work-life challenges, dependency, and/or stress-related issues.

Evidence-based medicine. A methodology for evaluating the validity of research in clinical medicine and applying the results to the care of individual patients.

Formulary. In medicine, a listing of prescription drugs approved for use.

Health Plan Employer Data and Information Set (HEDIS). Sponsored and maintained by NCQA, HEDIS is a set of standardized performance measures for a reliable comparison of the performance of managed health care programs.

Health promotion. Activities and support systems that assist individuals in taking greater responsibility for their own health maintenance and the appropriate use of health services.

Health and productivity management. The study of the relationship between health risks/status and targeted interventions and health care costs, disability, and productivity measures such as absenteeism, presenteeism, and work output.

Health risk appraisal (HRA). Questionnaires that use special rules (e.g., algorithms) to analyze health-related measures in order to identify current risk factors and their association with mortality or to future health problems (morbidity).

Health Reimbursement Account (HRA). Used to fund a portion of a high deductible, health plan (HDHP). Rollover permitted, but may be limited by employer. Account is not portable.

Health Savings Account (HSA). Used to fund a portion of a high deductible, health plan (HDHP). Employee and/or employer funded. Pretax employee contributions. Portable if employee terminates. Rollover allowed, effective savings vehicle for retirement.

Indirect Health Care Costs. The additional cost impact associated with health-related events such as short- and long-term disability, absenteeism, and presenteeism.

Medical self-care. Using information, skills, and supports to determine the appropriate use of medical resources (e.g., emergency room and ambulatory care) or other options (e.g., self-treatment) when a health problem occurs.

Multitiered Pharmacy (Formulary) Plans. The categorization of specific medications based on cost and use. For example, a three-tiered pharmacy plan is usually organized with generic drugs as tier-one; preferred-brand drugs as tier-two; and nonpreferred brand drugs as tier-three. Graduated copays or coinsurance (lowest to highest) are charged respective to each tier.

Non-Formulary. Brand name medications that are not listed on the health plan formulary.

Pay-for-performance. Incentive arrangement between health plans (or employer) and providers to comply with established evidence-based standards of care.

Pharmacy Benefit Manager (PBM). An information-based, clinically oriented service organization that manages prescription benefits for other companies, including employers, managed care organizations, and health insurance companies.

Population management. The integration and delivery of appropriate health management services and supports across the continuum of care.

Predictive modeling. An evaluation system that uses artificial intelligence (AI) applications prospectively to identify future trends in medical utilization and related costs and the potential effects (e.g., cost-savings) of different intervention scenarios.

Presenteeism. The measurement of on-the-job work impairment. Presenteeism takes into account that a worker who is physically present may not be fully engaged in work activities because of a health problem or other work/life issues.

Quality of Care. The degree to which health care is expected to increase the likelihood of desired health outcomes and is consistent with standards of health care.

Value-based benefits design. The planning and administration of employee health benefits based on the specific needs of the organization (and the individual) and the potential value that the benefit offering provides. As such, the total value and total return (e.g., improved clinical outcomes, improved productivity, lower total health-related costs) is weighed against the initial investment of a targeted intervention (e.g., lowering copays for a specific drug class).

Source: *Human Capital, Your Greatest Asset: Building Effective Strategies to Protect, Support and Enhance Workplace Health and Productivity.* GlaxoSmithKline. Philadelphia, Penna. 2005.[64]

John J. Mahoney, M.D.

John J. (Jack) Mahoney is the Corporate Medical Director and Global Health Care Management Director at Pitney Bowes. He is responsible for strategic health initiatives including designing health benefits for employees, and integrating disability, disease management, and wellness initiatives. He has oversight for all clinical support services.

Jack received his undergraduate degree from Boston College and his Medical Degree from the Medical College of Virginia. He also received a Masters Degree in Public Health from UCLA.

David Hom

David Hom is a Vice President in the Strategic H.R. Initiatives Department at Pitney Bowes in Stamford, Connecticut. Since 1992, Mr. Hom has been responsible for developing a nationally recognized and award-winning integrated health care strategy that focuses on increased employee productivity through disease, disability and demand management programs.

Mr. Hom received his undergraduate degree in economics from the State University of New York at Albany and his MBA degree from Hofstra University.